*Where Has
Grandpa Gone?*

Also by Dr. Ruth Kopp—
Encounter With Terminal Illness

Where Has Grandpa Gone?

HELPING CHILDREN COPE WITH GRIEF AND LOSS

Ruth Kopp

With Read-aloud Section for Children: "Mommy, What Does It Mean to Die?"

ZONDERVAN PUBLISHING HOUSE OF THE ZONDERVAN CORPORATION
GRAND RAPIDS, MICHIGAN 49506

Library of Congress Cataloging in Publication Data

Kopp, Ruth.
     Where has grandpa gone?

     Bibliography: p.
     Includes index.
     1. Grief in children. 2. Children and death.
I. Title.
BF723.G75K66   1983   155.9'37   83-10496
ISBN 0-310-41611-6

Printed in the United States of America

83 84 85 86 87 88 / 9 8 7 6 5 4 3 2

To my children,
Juanita and Jim,
without whom this book would
have been impossible

CONTENTS

Where Has Grandpa Gone?

Mommy, What Does It Mean to Die?

ACKNOWLEDGMENTS

THIS BOOK WAS CONCEIVED and nurtured within my family, in the conversations my husband and I have had with our children regarding separation, loss, and grief, and in our firsthand experience with the children's grief. I am grateful to the many families of my patients who have shared their children with me as they went through their own separation, loss, and grief.

I am also deeply indebted to Jan Ierulli for many hours of her time and for her ability to listen sensitively. Without her help, the ideas in this book might have stayed in my head and heart and never have made it out through the typewriter and onto the page! I am also grateful to Cheryl Forbes for her help in shaping these ideas into a book.

Perhaps my deepest debt of gratitude is to my husband, without whom I would not be the person I am, and without whose love and support I would never be able to write.

Where Has Grandpa Gone?

1 UNDERSTANDING DEATH

DRIVING HOME ONE DAY, I saw a dead rabbit in the street in front of our home. It was stiff, motionless, and cold. I pulled it out of the street and into the snowbank beside the sidewalk. Before long, all the neighborhood children knew about the dead rabbit and had come to look at it and touch it.

Children have many contacts with death, even before they reach school age. They see it on television; they hear about it in the news; it is announced in church and discussed by the adults around them. There are dead rabbits and squirrels in the road, dead birds on the lawn.

We cannot shield our children from death. We can't prevent their hearing about it and seeing it. In recent years I have kept track of the deaths my children have encountered as part of our private lives—deaths not connected with my husband's medical practice or mine. The following list, though incomplete, serves to illustrate the variety of our children's experiences with death:

—Jimmy had two classmates whose fathers died while he was in nursery school, and one classmate in kindergarten whose father died;

—Twin babies were stillborn to the mother of one of Juanita's friends in first grade;

—A friend of mine came over for coffee to discuss the suicide of one of her neighbors, a young man with children aged five and seven; my children were in and out of the kitchen during the conversation and heard about the suicide;

—A young mother shot her six- and nine-year-old daughters and herself; this suicide and murder were discussed in church, at home, and in other places where my children overheard;

9

—A teen-age girl was murdered after work one evening; the murder was widely publicized by the news media and was the topic of many conversations;

—The children's choir director in our church and a retired volunteer at the children's school both died of cancer within a year;

—Friends of our children have had grandparents, friends, and pets die; some of these were deaths from "natural causes" and some were accidents;

—Of our pets, an African millipede, a garter snake, numerous guppies, and two litters of baby mice have died.

Each of these experiences has given our children an opportunity to develop their understanding of death. In these situations our children have had to face the fact of death and deal with it. Little by little, children learn that all living things die. This eventually brings them to the point of realizing that their grandparents, parents, and friends will also die. Eventually they realize that they too will die someday. Studies show that children begin to think about death and develop defenses against the idea of death as early as the age of three.

We can allow our children to develop their ideas of death and its meaning by themselves, or we can choose to be consciously involved in the process. Consciously or not, we will influence our children's ideas and understanding by our own behavior. Even if we choose not to talk with them about death and its meaning, our own feelings, reactions, fears, and hopes will be communicated to our children.

It is easy to decide to help our children learn about death "later." We feel that we have plenty of time. We hesitate to introduce the painful subjects of death and grief to young children, and we may avoid dealing with the subjects when they come up naturally, in hopes that the children will forget about them and be spared dealing with them. But being prepared to face death and the loss it brings means being prepared *now*. If we wait until later, we may find that we are forced to deal with ideas and attitudes that have already developed. We may also discover that "later" is a time of personal bereavement in which we must deal with our own loss and feelings of grief. In a time of bereavement, the emotional burden of our own grief and our children's makes the task of teaching more difficult. Waiting until our children are older and—we imagine—

better prepared to deal with loss and grief only makes our teaching task more complex.

Understanding death begins with recognition of its physical aspects. This is what children learn first about death. In their first experience—the dead rabbit in the road, the dead fish in the aquarium—the most obvious thing is the physical stillness: The rabbit doesn't hop away any more; the fish floats, belly up, on the top of the water, instead of darting around with the other fish.

Young children know how to "play dead." By age three or four, they know that when you're dead you must lie still, close your eyes, and stop talking. If the "dead" child gets up, walks around, talks, or opens his eyes, the other children become angry, shouting, "You can't do that! You're dead!"

In children's games, however, death is easily reversible. As the game continues, the "dead" child gets up and takes his part with the other children. He once again walks, talks, and jumps. Death is not a permanent fact for children under five. Faced with a dead pet, they may ask, "When will he stop being dead?"

UNDERSTANDING TIME

The idea of death as permanent requires an understanding of time, particularly the concept of the future. This understanding develops gradually in a child. A five-year-old may shout angrily, "I hate you forever!" yet come back in an hour or two with hugs and kisses, his "forever" hate totally forgotten.

An infant exists totally in the present. He is aware only of his current feelings and sensations. At this early age, it is probable that the infant experiences the absence of any important person in his life as the "death" of that person. The absence of his mother is total absence; the infant has no conscious recollections of the mother or any expectations of her return.

Through the repetition of a daily routine, and through the coming and going of his mother and other people, an infant begins to form a primitive sense of time. He can remember things that happened and begins to rely on repetition and recurrence in his schedule. The routine of meals, baths, outings, and naps becomes familiar. As he is able to remember, he begins to look forward as well. He expects the routine to continue and gains a rudimentary idea of "future."

Game's Progress

"Peekaboo," an almost universal game played with infants and young children, is a first step in a child's learning that people can go away and come back. Parents, friends, and older children play peekaboo with the baby as early as six or seven months of age. First the face is hidden from the baby's sight with the hands; then the hands are dropped and the person "reappears"! Very soon the child learns to hide his own face and laughs delightedly as he too vanishes and reappears.

The game progresses from hiding the face with the hand to hiding the entire body with a cover or blanket. "Where's my baby?" mother cries as she covers up the baby. Then she lifts a corner of the blanket, smiling, and exclaims, "There's my baby!" Later mother begins hiding in a corner, behind a curtain, behind a chair. "Where's mommy?" she asks, and baby begins to look for her. "Here's mommy!" mother says, and out she comes from her hiding place.

About the age of eighteen months, the infant begins to trust that people who go away will return. At first the child protests violently when his mother leaves. But through games, daily routines, and mother's comings and goings, the child comes to expect mother's return. Within a few months this trust becomes strong enough for the child to allow his mother to leave without the violent protests. He comes to depend on the routine in his schedule and expects it to continue. He becomes able to trust the patterns emerging in his life.

After this, the child's understanding of time grows. It is learned in terms of the important activities in his life. As he remembers the past, he is gradually able to anticipate the future.

Discovering "Tomorrow"

Anyone who has told a three- or four-year-old that she is going to a birthday party "tomorrow" knows the exasperation of trying to help the child understand what "tomorrow" means. "Is it tomorrow yet?" the child asks. "No, it's just afternoon. After this we have dinner. Then you take your bath and brush your teeth. Then you go to bed. After you go to sleep, when you wake up, it will be tomorrow." At this point the child may ask for her dinner, bath, and bed immediately, or she may lie down, close her eyes, get up, and say, "I slept. Now is it tomorrow?"

Little by little a child's sense of time matures. Monday is the beginning of the week; Sunday means church; Friday is the beginning of the weekend; Saturday morning is for watching cartoons. The concept of time begins as the routine of the day learned by the one- to three-year-old: breakfast, lunch, nap, dinner. The cycle of the week is learned as daily routine varies regularly, between ages four and seven. The child gains a sense of security through the dependability of certain things happening at certain times, on certain days. This helps him develop an idea of the future—the sense that next Sunday will be like last Sunday and the Sunday before that. The memory of Sunday school last week and the previous week helps the child to look forward to next Sunday and Sunday school. The future begins to have meaning in terms of familiar activities and established routine.

It seems to take endless repetitions for children to grasp the meaning of time. My friend Sybil, who is six, spends Tuesday afternoons with me. It seems that every week we go through the same ritual. As she leaves my home, she will ask, "When do I come to your house again?"

"Next Tuesday," I answer her.

"Is that tomorrow?"

"No, tomorrow is Wednesday. Wednesdays are for the potluck. Then comes Thursday, then Friday."

"Then is it Tuesday? Then do you keep me?" she asks.

"No, not yet. After Friday come Saturday and Sunday. That's the weekend and your mommy's home. After Sunday comes Monday. On Mondays you go to Latch Key."

"And then is it Tuesday? Then do I come to your house?"

"Yes, after Monday comes Tuesday, and Tuesday is our day together."

Cycle of the Year

Gradually the child expands his sense of time to include the seasons and the cycle of the year. Somewhere between the ages of seven and nine a child's concept of time has developed to the point that he will have some understanding of death as permanent, realizing that it has an impact on his future as well as being a fact in the present.

I can remember the near-ritual question-and-answer sessions

with my own children, establishing the cycle of the year. Perhaps soon after Christmas, Jimmy would say, "Next comes my birthday." We would then go through the cycle of our own personal year in terms of Uncle's birthday (January), Grandma and Grandpa Kopp's birthdays and daddy's birthday (February), St. Patrick's Day (March), Passover and Easter (March or April), Mother's Day (May), Grandpa Lewshenia's birthday and mommy's birthday, and both grandmas' and grandpas' wedding anniversaries (June), Jimmy's birthday and Independence Day (July), and on through the rest of the year. The holidays and birthdays that are important to us give the cycle of the year meaning in our family and in the lives of our friends.

FORMING RELATIONSHIPS

Even while the child is learning about time, he is developing his ability to form relationships. The development of a sense of himself and a sense of other people as separate from himself is the first step.

The infant spends much of his first year exploring and claiming his own body. At birth he is not aware of himself as a separate person, nor is he aware of anyone or anything in the world as separate from himself. Then he discovers his mouth, his head, his hands and feet, fingers and toes. He learns to hold his head up and move it. He learns to put things into his mouth. He learns to use his hands to pick up objects and drop them. Later he learns to sit, then stand, then gain enough control over his body to crawl and to walk.

As he discovers the parts of his body and gradually brings them under his control, he also becomes aware that there are things which are not a part of him. He begins to relate to people and things separate from himself. This first happens about the age of six to nine months, when he makes the distinction between himself and his mother. At first, when he cries from hunger and discomfort, he does not associate the subsequent relief with a person; later he learns that this relief is brought by someone who comes in response to his cry. He learns to smile and finds that people around him respond to his smiles. He hears others talking to him; he begins to make sounds and discovers that others respond to his sounds. Later he learns that certain sounds are associated with certain things, and gradually he learns to talk, using words to reach others and to interact with them.

A young child is very much the center of his own world. At first he is unaware of the presence of anyone else. As he learns about himself, he finds the limits of his own person and the difference between himself and other selves. However, he is still almost totally absorbed in himself, relating to others as they are able to respond to him or to fill his needs.

Varieties of Nonself

Once the child has made the distinction between himself and others, he is able to distinguish among the other people. As a rule, all other people are interchangeable to an infant during the first year of life; he recognizes the difference between self and nonself, but does not yet know that there are also varieties of nonself. Between the ages of eight and ten months he learns to recognize his mother and loses his ready acceptance of strangers. By his first birthday he is usually able to recognize the constant figures in his world: Mommy, daddy, brothers, and sisters. As with all developmental features, this timetable may vary with the infant's personality, some children learning to recognize mother as early as three or four months old.

As the child becomes "self-propelled," his world expands. He comes to recognize more people and learns more of his environment. His major energy, however, is still engaged in learning to control his body and its functions. The toddler is busy perfecting the skills of walking and running and is learning to control his bowels and bladder. He has a little—but very little—energy left over to invest in other people and relationships. His acts of love and spontaneous giving are few and short-lived, interspersed with his need to explore and master the world. The love he feels for others is largely made up of his dependency on them. Two- and three-year-olds may play side by side with others, but they rarely play together.

By the age of three, the child has gained a degree of mastery over his own body. He can walk, run, feed himself (after a fashion); he is toilet-trained; he is beginning to communicate with others by talking. As he becomes more confident of his control of his body and its functions, he turns his attention to the world outside himself. He begins to experiment with his ability to control the world in which he lives. He tries out his influence on the people around him. By using his body and his newfound power of words, he sets out to expand the limits of his control. Using the word *No* is one way he expresses his need to gain control.

About the age of five, the child enters a new period of fascination with his body. The child from five to seven is interested in the way his body works. He becomes interested in illness, accidents, and injuries. These unknowns are able to take control over the body he has so recently mastered and to change the way it responds to his ideas and wishes. Children at these ages tend to develop sympathetic symptoms when a sibling or friend is ill, or when they see a movie or television program that stresses a particular illness. A day or two after he saw the movie *Joni,* Jimmy fell and had a "paralyzed" arm for twenty-four hours!

A NEW SENSE OF DEATH

As the child tries to understand his body and the meaning of illness, his understanding of death develops in a new way. Ideas as well as things and events are personified in his mind. He has not yet made a clear distinction between living and nonliving things. Most children between two and six years old see everything that moves and has activity as being alive and personal. They may have difficulty understanding the qualitative difference between the "life" in the actions of a mechanical toy and the life in the movements of a pet. Toys, stuffed animals, and even blankets have names, feelings, and personality. Gradually the child comes to recognize the difference between his interactions with people and animals and his ability to use and manipulate things.

The young child, living in a world of persons, tends to personify abstract ideas and events as well. There is a similarity between his understanding and that of the primitive tribes who see love, fertility, death, the wind, the rain, the sun, and the seasons as deities. These deities must be dealt with in a personal way, either to win their favor or to pacify their wrath. So the young child personifies death, understanding it as an awesome supermonster that kills. The three- or four-year-old has no concept of "dying"; his understanding of death is limited to the idea of "killing."

As the child becomes aware of death, he realizes that people and animals can "be killed." Death is a powerful being; it can come at will and remove people and pets that the child loves. He realizes that his family, his pets, or his friends could "be killed"—as he himself could be. With this realization, the child begins to develop mechanisms to cope with the monster death, to protect himself and those he loves from being killed. A fear of death seems to be present as soon as a child becomes aware of death; there seems to be no age at which the idea is accepted calmly or matter-of-factly. As soon as he understands that living things die, he begins to protest against death and especially against his own. Awareness brings the strong feelings that "I don't want to die!"

One five-year-old came home from Sunday school in tears and informed her mother, "I'm not going back there!" The girl had changed classes at her fifth birthday. She had always enjoyed Sunday school before this, so her mother was surprised.

"Why don't you want to go back? Why don't you like your new class?"

"They said that if you believe in Jesus you can go to heaven when you die. I don't want to die! And I don't want to go back there, where they talk about dying!"

Defenses Against Death

An early defense children use against death is their "blanket." This blanket is very important, representing security and stability. The child sees it as an extension of himself and turns to it for comfort. Part of the blanket's role is to hide the child when he is in distress and to comfort him when he feels hurt or insecure. Up to age three or four, the child handles external threats, including the threat of death, by hiding himself physically, under his blanket, in his mother's lap, or behind his mother or father.

From ages four to about six or seven the child tends to use fantasy, magic, and wishful thinking to protect himself. Jimmy was totally involved with the superheroes of his cartoons at that stage. He spent most of his free time making costumes and inventing elaborate stories of death and destruction in which he was the hero and saved himself and everyone else. He was Batman, Superman, Lightning Man, and other powerful superheroes in turn. From make-believe games Jimmy gradually moved to weight lifting, exercises, and running. He was no longer content to fantasize the superhero—he wanted to become one. He continually asked me how soon I thought he would be the strongest man in the world or

17

the fastest runner. His fantasies were no longer adequate for coping with death and destruction; he wanted to regain control of his world.

Jimmy's total absorption with superheroes worried me until I realized that this fantasy world of his was, and to some extent still is, one of his defenses against the idea of death. If he can be strong enough and fast enough to be a superhero he can save himself and those he loves from dying. The monster Death will be no match for him. Fantasies of superstrength or superspeed provide children with protection from the enemy. These can alleviate the pain and fear of knowing that the people they love, and they themselves, may "be killed."

This phase of understanding death coincides with a child's seeking to learn how his body works. His awareness of health, illness, accident, and injury is accompanied by concern for health, strength, diet, and exercise. His protection shifts from fantasy to the tangible, physical world. (This is true not only for children. One adult defense against the idea of aging, serious illness, or death lies in physical fitness and concern for diet. The current national attention given to fitness may arise in part from resistance to the thought of our own death, encouraged in a society that reveres youthfulness.)

The child's new, more materialist attitude toward death is reinforced by the adults around him. Parents begin to stress good diet, enough sleep, safety on the playground. These messages are echoed at school and in the "health commercials" on television and in books: "If you want to grow up big and strong, you will eat right, get enough sleep, brush your teeth." "Look both ways when crossing the street." "Keep your kite away from power lines."

The possibility of illness or injury surrounds the five-to-seven-year-old: "Wear your coat or you'll freeze to death!" "Don't ride your bike in the street!" "Don't swim in strange lakes!"

As the child's access to the physical world expands and he includes school, church, and his neighborhood in the territory he may explore and wander, parents set up new limits in the form of rules and commands. The vast majority of these rules involve the child's health and safety, either implicitly or explicitly. Small wonder that the child becomes preoccupied with his health and safety!

The Second Coming

In the midst of this materialist attitude, however, there may also be an abstract, uniquely Christian defense against the idea of death. Both my children have used their understanding of Jesus Christ's return to earth for protection. One day Juanita abruptly asserted, "I'd rather be second."

I couldn't fathom what was going on in her mind. "What do you mean, 'second'?"

"Well, those who have died will get their new bodies first when Jesus comes back," she said. "I'd rather be second and get my new body later. I don't want to have to die."

Jimmy has repeatedly told me that Jesus will come back before he dies, and he won't have to die. (He is willing to concede that I might have to die, since I'm so old!) One night we were talking about the possibility of his being away from home.

"If I were gone for a week would you miss me?" he asked.

"Yes, I'd miss you," I replied.

"Would you cry?"

"I don't know. Maybe. I think I could manage to get along without you for a week."

"Well, if I were gone for two weeks, would you cry? Three weeks? A year?"

"Yes, if you were gone for two or three weeks, I'd miss you a lot. I might even cry."

"If I died, would you come to my funeral?"

"Of course! And I would cry, too! I'd be the chief mourner at your funeral. Where would we bury you, if you died? Would you want to be in the columbarium at church?"

"I'm not going to be buried!"

"Why not?"

"If I died tonight, Jesus would come back tomorrow, so you wouldn't have to bury me. Jesus will come back before I am buried."

At seven, Jimmy realized he would die someday. But he hated the thought of dying! Although he accepts to a degree the real probability of his own death, he still fights against this truth. Part of the meaning that Christ has in Jimmy's life is as a protector against death.

THE INTELLECTUAL PLANE

As a child comes to understand that death isn't just an accident and that people die even if they are not "killed," he tends to move to another type of defense. He turns his interest to the outside world on an intellectual plane. He now begins a serious attempt to enter and master the world of facts and ideas.

The child of eight to eleven is vitally concerned with the reasons for things. These are the children who drive parents crazy in their fascination with trivia and details. In regard to death, these children ask, Why? What happened? What does that mean? Why did Grandpa get sick? Why do people die of leukemia? What is a heart attack? Why do heart attacks happen? Why do people die of heart attacks? The child becomes concerned with death and many other concepts on an intellectual and rational level, largely ignoring the emotions involved. A rational approach to frightening subjects can be a means of protection against fear and anxiety.

Juanita, who was nine, was at this point in her development. Jimmy, at age seven, was in transition to this way of coping, with an overlap between his desire to be strong enough, smart enough, and fast enough to defeat death and a rational approach to death in looking for reasons and explanations.

Exploring the world on an intellectual plane leaves the preadolescent with the emotional energy to invest in relationships. From ages seven to eleven or twelve is the time for "best friends," "favorite" teachers, and other pleasurable relationships. The tie between the parent and the child can take on many aspects of friendship, with shared books, ideas, and projects. The child has time and energy for "secret" treats for those he loves, surprise acts of thoughtfulness and caring, and spontaneous generosity.

Because the child has carved out a place for himself in his world and has a certain amount of independence and skill, he can form friendships that are less needy and dependent. He no longer has to use all his emotional energy in learning to know and control his body. He can be more relaxed in his approach to mastering his world. He can freely share himself and his possessions, confident of what is his and under his control. He is in a position for love to become more of a mutual relationship; he has something to offer others, as well as needing to receive from them.

DEATH OF A LOVED ONE

The death of a close relative at this time can be very painful to bear.

Kathy's grandfather died when she was eleven. Because both of Kathy's parents worked, she had spent a lot of time with grandma and grandpa. She went to their home before school to wait for the school bus; if she overslept and was late, grandpa drove her to school. She came home to grandma and grandpa. Grandpa drove her to her ballet lessons, her piano lessons, and Girl Scouts. He picked her up at school if she was sick. He took her shopping, played games with her, and helped her with her homework. He was often the first person to see her report card or to hear about a misunderstanding with her best friend.

When grandpa died, Kathy's life changed radically. Who would drive her to school now if she missed the bus? Who would help her with her homework, take her to her lessons, share her secret jokes? Would grandma move away, now that grandpa was dead?

For Kathy, these questions represented the meaning of grandpa's death in her life. Although she knew about his death as soon as it happened, it still took time to test its reality by finding him gone when she came home from school, by going to her lessons with someone else, by finding grandma alone when she ran over to their home. The first Easter after grandpa's death brought new grief; the first trip Kathy's family took without grandpa was a new reminder of his death; the first Christmas without grandpa was a mixture of sadness and joy for the whole family.

Within a year after her grandfather's death, Kathy had probably replenished most of the losses represented in her grandfather's death. She accepted and adjusted to the changes in her daily routine. She is able to remember him with affection and joy, although there is still the pain of missing him.

The meaning of the death of a loved one to a child will vary with the stage of his emotional development. His understanding of a particular death will depend on the degree to which he understands death in general. The fact of the permanence of death and its meaning for the future depend on his idea of time. Other factors influencing the child's response are the role the person played in his life, the amount of time spent together, and the way in which the others involved with the child respond to the loss, especially their response to the child's personal loss.

When our friend John Hillis died, Jimmy, who was five, periodically reminded us that John was dead and couldn't be part of the things our family shared with his family. "John Hillis won't come over and sing Christmas carols with us," he said in early December. At Easter time, "John Hillis won't be here for our Passover dinner." In the summer, "John Hillis can't come to my birthday party this year and play baseball with us." As we went through the first year after John's death, Jimmy was gradually able to absorb its reality and meaning in relating John's absence to the times when he would normally have been at our house.

A child needs to test the death of a friend, family member, or beloved pet against the context and fabric of his own life for it to become real and meaningful. He learns by associating new ideas with familiar things. Just as the meaning of time is learned first in terms of activities that are meaningful to the child, such as Sybil's coming to my house on Tuesdays or Jimmy's watching cartoons on Saturday mornings, so too the meaning of death is grasped by relating it to the familiar routine and day-to-day experience.

It is important to deal with the changes in schedule and routine for a child who has lost a loved one. These details, sometimes seemingly trivial, signify the child's ability to accept the meaning of this death in his own life. They also represent security and continuity for him.

Yet these changes in schedule and routine are not the most important part of dealing with death. Death means loss; the feeling that accompanies loss is grief. Although the child may be able to grasp the physical fact of death and may be able to deal intellectually with the changes it will mean in his life, this is different from feeling and dealing with grief.

By far the strongest impact of death is emotional. Far greater than the questions of "Who will drive me to school?" or "Will you get married again, daddy?" is the devastating feeling of grief over a loss. We need to prepare our children for these feelings—feelings that range from numbness to a great aching void inside, from disbelief to a burning rage.

Most of this book will deal with grief, its various expressions, and children's and adults' ways of dealing with it. The patterns suggested in our discussion of grief are general, even when they deal with a particular age or developmental stage. Each child, like every adult, will have a personal pattern of grieving. Children vary in their ability to understand the meaning of their loss, in the time it takes them to test the reality of it, and in the ways in which they cope with their grief. A child who is grieving is unique, and adults' responses to him must be sensitive to the patterns that will serve him best.

2 / WHAT IS GRIEF?

JIMMY, JUANITA, AND I were talking about the various ways people grieve. I asked them to help me with this book, to tell me how they felt about matters of death and grief. Jimmy sat quietly for a minute, obviously deep in thought. He was five.

"Mommy," Jimmy said finally, "I've lost six people who were close to me, and I've never grieved. What's wrong with me?"

This question startled me. How had he come to the conclusion that he had never grieved? What made him feel there was "something wrong" with him?

At least in part, Jimmy's idea that he had "never grieved" arose in the differences among the members of the family. Tears come less easily to Jimmy than to Juanita, their father, and me. Jimmy may have the same feelings the rest of us have, but he expresses himself differently. Whatever tears may be there are usually hidden deep inside. Instead of crying, Jimmy talks loudly and rapidly, paces up and down, or races around the house. He almost has to pick a fight, get himself yelled at, or misbehave before he is able to cry for a "legitimate" reason.

One of the primary learning tasks of a child is to distinguish between right and wrong. By age five or six, most children develop a strong sense of morality and have a conviction that there is a "right" and "wrong" way to do everything, from setting the table to saying their prayers. Only a small part of this learning comes through direct teaching; most of it is gained by observation of the way others, especially people older than the child, behave. Children form their ideas about the rightness or wrongness of behavior by observing the adults they love and trust, and older children.

25

Jimmy had formed his ideas of the "right" way to grieve on the basis of his observation of other people. He had been to funerals and visitations; he had visited families after the death of a loved one; he had seen Jim, Juanita, and me respond to the death of people we cared about. When he looked at himself, his feelings and behavior did not seem the same as others'. So he concluded that he had never grieved, and this meant there was something wrong with him.

OBSERVING GRIEF

How do we learn about grief? What is it? After hours of thinking about grief and discussing it with others, I have come to several conclusions. Grief is a complex made up of many feelings, physical reactions, and thoughts. Grief finds many means of expression in our behavior. Grief is something we learn about largely by observation and inference, rarely by direct teaching.

C. S. Lewis begins his book, *A Grief Observed*—a diary of his experiences and feelings after his wife's death—with the words, "No one ever told me. . . ." His words are true of the majority of us. No one ever tells us about grief. It was never offered to me as a course in high school, college, or medical school; it was never the subject of a class discussion or the assigned topic for a theme; it was never part of the vigorous conversations that characterized our home while I was growing up.

Only recently have I even begun to discuss grief with others and to attend seminars and lectures on grief. These seminars have been largely an outgrowth of the recent focus on work with the terminally ill and the needs of the dying. There is still a relative scarcity of literature and studies available on grief, bereavement, and the work of mourning, although this is beginning to change. Many of the articles about grief are in specialized literature, such as nursing journals, Hospice newsletters, and psychology and psychiatry journals; therefore, this information is largely unavailable to the general public.

My first ideas of grief were shaped by what I observed in the behavior of people grieving for a loved one. These ideas were altered and expanded by reading. Yet, even in reading, much of my learning about grief came from observing the grieving behavior of the characters in the books. I also found that much of my knowledge remained on a feeling or instinctive level; only as I tried to discuss grief with others were these feelings finally put into words.

Learning about grief is a lifelong process. It goes hand in hand with learning about love. Just as there are many facets and degrees of love, so too there are many facets and degrees of grief.

Learning Through Inference

Since grief is essentially a complex of different feelings, it cannot be observed directly. Grief is the sum total of the feelings we have when we suffer a loss. What we learn about grief through observing others is the behavior that expresses the feelings. We infer from the behavior what those feelings are. These inferences may or may not be accurate. The same behavior can result from various feelings; tears may express joy or relief or sadness or anger or frustration or despair; laughter may be bitter as well as joyful. Nonchalant behavior can mean indifference, but it can also mask intense feelings of excitement or anger.

Children learn very early to associate tears with sadness, and sadness with grief. When Juanita's pet African millipede died, Jimmy knew she was grieving; Juanita wept buckets of tears, locked herself in her room, and refused her dinner. Jimmy could see a familiar pattern of grief in her behavior. On the other hand, I shed no tears, stayed in the kitchen, and ate my dinner.

"Mommy, aren't you sad that Juanita's millipede died?" Jimmy asked me.

"Yes, I am. I'm going to miss it too."

He looked at me and commented, "Well, it doesn't seem as if you're sad. You didn't even cry."

At that point Jimmy was expressing the belief "no tears mean no grief." It was the same perspective that he expressed later on as *his* having "never grieved."

We learn to expect certain behavior to express grief. The kind of behavior expected is determined by the standards of the family, the church, and the social environment to which we belong. The weeping and wailing and physical contortions of a Haitian funeral procession would seem bizarre and out of place at Fourth Presbyterian Church on Michigan Avenue in Chicago; the behavior at a funeral in the Chicago church might not even be recognized as grief by a visitor from Port-au-Prince. Blacks, Whites, Hispanics, Italians, Germans, Englishmen, and Slavic peoples all vary in their ideas of appropriate and acceptable grief behavior. Loud, hysterical sobbing may be the pattern in one family, while a few silent tears, gently shed into a tiny lace handkerchief, may be the rule in another. Learning about grief by observation requires that we take these family and cultural standards into consideration.

PHYSICAL REACTIONS

Grief behavior is an expression of basically two sets of physical reactions. The psychological terms used to define these physical reactions are "anxiety" and "depression." In the language of the psychologist, the grief reaction shows all the symptoms of an "agitated depression."

Peter Harris developed Hodgkin's disease, a cancer involving the lymph nodes, in his early twenties, before he married and had children. Although he had several good remissions (periods when the disease was inactive) lasting for months and years, his children were always aware of his illness. When he finally did not respond to further treatment, his children were told. They could see that he was getting thinner and weaker. John, age eight, and Sarah, age four, were included as much as possible in the final events of Peter's life. Peter was cared for at home until his condition made this too difficult.

When Peter died, his son, John, cried a little. John attended the visitation and funeral with great interest, spending time looking at his father's body, but showing no observable signs of "sadness." However, in the following weeks there were several marked changes in John's behavior. He would awaken early in the morning, at 4:30 or 5:00, and roam around the house. He had difficulty getting to sleep at night. He moved restlessly from one place to another, from one project to another, rarely able to settle down for more than five minutes at a time. He would tell his mother that he was starved, then eat two or three bites of his meal, push away his plate, and say he was full. He held himself stiffly and walked with an appearance of having a lot of pent-up energy.

Signs of Anxiety

John's grieving showed many of the physical signs of anxiety. Anxiety is a lot like fear. There is a sense of vague uneasiness, restlessness, nervousness, an inability to concentrate. The grieving person will look stiff and rigid, and he may have a set or even fierce expression on his face. He may move somewhat awkwardly, with jerky, nervous movements.

The anxiety of grief may be felt physically in the pit of the stomach as a gnawing emptiness or a fluttery sensation of "butterflies." Like John, the grieving person may feel "starved," yet be unable to eat. Or this person, child or adult, may eat continually and nervously, attempting to fill up the emptiness inside. Another common feeling is the "lump in the throat," accompanied by difficulty in swallowing.

Other signs of grief in which anxiety predominates are stomach aches, stomach cramps, nausea, or diarrhea. A child may breathe quickly and shallowly and complain that he feels "smothered" or that he can't "catch his breath." As in John's case, grief may cause changes in sleeping habits.

Signs of Depression

We are more accustomed to associate the signs of depression with the idea of grief. The depressed child will move slowly, speak slowly or not at all, and seem not to hear when he is spoken to. He may cry easily and for no apparent reason. He may find it hard to make decisions or choices, acting as if he doesn't care about what he eats or what he does.

The grieving child in whom depression is most evident will walk slowly with shoulders down and head bent. He will sit slumped and still in a chair. His face will have almost no expression, and his expression will not change as he talks, moves, or listens to others.

Depression as a part of grief also affects sleeping and eating habits. The child may act and feel tired all the time; he may go to bed early and have difficulty getting up. He may lose his appetite and show no interest even in his favorite foods.

The physical signs of grief will be some combination of the signs of anxiety and depression. The grieving child may walk slowly, with head down and shoulders bent, or he may walk stiffly, with a nervous energy. His face may be nearly expressionless, or his expression may be rigid and set. He will probably show some change in his sleeping and eating, doing both either more or less than usual. He will probably show a lack of concentration and an inability to make decisions.

In the first days of grief, a person, whether child or adult, will probably show changes from his typical behavior. He may abandon activities that interested him before, such as reading, working on a collection, or sports; he may replace former activities with a flurry of new ones, or he may withdraw from most activities altogether. In the event of a severe loss, the child will probably withdraw at least temporarily from the activities that have formed the pattern of his "normal" life.

Because we generally associate the word *grief* with sadness, we may not look for the physical signs and expressions that we do not associate with "sadness" in our own minds. Even if we notice these signs and behavior, we may not recognize them as part of the grief process. In observing the grief of others we tend to notice and "learn" only those behaviors that conform with our own ideas of sadness, thereby limiting and distorting our understanding of grief.

Moreover, we limit our understanding by reserving the word for experiences with death. We rarely recognize the grief that results from other forms of loss. Yet grief is really the word applied to everything that we feel in response to any loss. Just as our losses vary in degree and importance to us, so the grief we feel varies in intensity and duration. There is as much variation in grief as there are varieties of attachments to people, places, and things.

Our observation of the grief of others can add to our understanding, but what we learn this way is limited and can be misleading. The most accurate teacher is experience. If we remember that grief is what we call the reaction to any loss—not just loss through death—we realize that we have many opportunities in daily living to learn about grief experientially. There is no need to manufacture opportunities for ourselves or our children. Every time we go through a separation or suffer a loss, we grieve. In so doing, we learn about the feelings of grief at first hand and develop our own patterns of grieving.

"LITTLE DEATHS"

These separations and losses that form a part of our day-to-day living are "little deaths." The "little deaths" may be the loss of an earring or a change of school; they come as the breaking of a lifelong friendship or a change of mailman. Through a variety of major and minor losses in daily life, we form the attitudes and coping mechanisms that become a personal pattern of grieving.

To illustrate the various parts of the typical grief response, I will cite several examples of "little death" situations with my children. These aspects of minor loss are comparable to the feelings we commonly experience, in greater magnitude, in the loss of a loved one or of something important to us.

During the summer that Juanita was seven, I had been speaking and lecturing in Dallas. One of my emphases was the subject of allowing our children to experience, feel, and deal with loss. While in Dallas, Juanita had bought a set of colorful plastic headbands. She especially liked the pink one, because pink is her favorite color.

Driving from Dallas to our home in Peoria, the children and I stopped at a recreation area in Oklahoma to swim and rest. Many miles after we left the place, there came a wail of anguish from the back seat. "Mommy, my headband is gone! The pink one! Can we go back and look for it?"

"Are you sure it's gone?" I half-turned in my seat to glance into the back. "Maybe it just fell on the floor or down behind the seat."

Juanita looked around a little. She was crying. "No, mommy, it isn't here!"

What should I do? Should I turn the car around and go back to look for it? Should I stop at the next town, find a dime store, and buy another pink headband?

"Mommy!" Juanita sobbed. "Please stop and buy me another pink headband!"

I remembered that Juanita was wearing her headband as she swam in the lake at the recreation center. She probably lost it in the water; if so, it would be impossible to find. In any case, we were twenty or more miles down the road by now and returning would delay us at least an hour.

"Honey, we can't go back," I told her. "It's too far, and it's very unlikely that we would find your headband anyway. Remember how muddy the lake was?"

"Well, can we stop and get another one, then?" she pleaded.

I considered this for a while. My own words, spoken just days before, about the importance of allowing our children to experience grief decided the issue. We would go on. "Honey, I'm sorry you lost your favorite headband. It was pretty, and you looked very nice in it. It's all right to cry about it. I'm sad you lost it, too. But right now, we can't stop and look for another one. We'll wait until we get home, then we'll see."

Disbelief and Denial

The loss of Juanita's headband was a "little death" for her. She and I reacted to this simple, everyday situation of loss in a typical way. The first feeling for both of us was disbelief. We didn't really believe it was gone. When she discovered that the headband was missing, Juanita searched through all her possessions for it. When she told me of the loss, I asked her to look for it again even though I knew she had worn it in the water.

Part of this disbelief was the impulse to go back to the recreation area and look for the headband. This too was a form of denial that the headband was gone: If we just went back, we thought subconsciously, we would find it right where we left it.

In this case the feeling of disbelief was fleeting. This initial denial was so slight that I wouldn't have recognized it unless I had been analyzing the loss. In our "little deaths," denial may be so brief that we don't even notice it; yet denial is a usual initial reaction. The greater the loss, the more pronounced the denial is likely to be, and the longer it will last, reoccurring over a period of days, weeks, or even months. The feelings "This isn't really happening" or "I'm dreaming this and will wake up soon" or "I can't believe it" are common.

Denial is a protective shield for our emotions, holding information of deep emotional impact away from us for a while. In a severe loss—the death of a parent, a home through fire, or a normal activity through severe illness or injury—the denial may be like a state of shock. The child (or adult) may appear to be dazed, finding it difficult to absorb information: what is happening, what people say, the present surroundings. He is unable to grasp the reality of the loss.

This buffer of shock or denial gives time to get together other mechanisms to cope with the emotional stress. As such, it is very useful. It can keep us from hasty, impulsive decisions and actions; it can numb our emotions for a while, allowing us to keep going, attend to details, and act rationally and objectively. Like the

Novocaine that allows us to have a diseased tooth extracted, it deadens our feelings; when the nerves recover from the Novocaine, some healing has already begun and the pain of the extraction is already less severe. By the time the shock of a personal loss wears off, some healing has taken place and the feelings of pain are reduced enough that we are capable of taking part in normal living.

We must realize that the time needed for this initial denial and shock varies from person to person, and even for one person the time will vary from loss to loss. Learning about grief is not merely a matter of discovering "normal" or "average" grief reactions and behavior; it means learning one's unique, personal way of grieving, discovering his own timetable, and finding his own strengths and abilities. As we teach our children, we need to be aware of their unique personalities and help them to discover their personal patterns of healthful grieving.

Children need time to test the reality of their loss before they can accept it and deal with it. Thus a child who has lost his "blankey" may ask for it time after time, even for a period of days, although he "knows" that it is gone. A three-or-four-year-old whose grandfather has died may ask over and over again to go to grandpa's house or to call grandpa on the telephone. Depending on the age of the child and especially on his grasp of the concept of the future, he may accept the fact of his grandfather's death after two or three attempts to call or visit; another may keep looking for grandpa off and on for a period of months. As parents we must be patient. We may need to repeat dozens of times that the blanket is lost or that grandpa is dead, as the children grapple with their need to test the loss and find it real. This can be very difficult, because as parents we wish to spare our children pain and sorrow.

It requires extra patience, moreover, when a child's loss is also a loss and source of grief for us. The child's testing of the loss accentuates our own loss and intensifies our feelings.

Immediate Replacement

Attempting to replace a lost object immediately with something identical or similar is another form of denial. It is easy to buy another ice cream cone to replace the one that fell, or to buy another headband for the lost one. Yet, if we deny to our children the experience of loss in relatively small matters, they will not learn how to deal with major loss and to endure grief. Instead, we will encourage them to avoid grief and deny the reality of the loss. Juanita wanted to stop and buy another headband immediately; this was an attempt to avoid the pain of the grief—another form of denial. Burying the feelings this way can sidetrack the work of mourning. It can leave us or our children no wiser for future instances of coping with loss and grief. It can even result in distortions of the grief process, with long-term emotional scars.

A similar coping mechanism—distraction—is often used by parents and other adults in dealing with children. This produces the same problems as replacement: distorting the grief process and leaving emotional scars, especially if the distraction is prolonged.

These mechanisms imply that nothing is special, that things are interchangeable. They declare that a new teddy bear is the same as the beloved, bedraggled animal the child has slept with for months; a new blanket is no different from the one that has been cuddled, dragged, and cried into for a year. The child's emotional investment in his toys and belongings is discounted if a lost toy or blanket is immediately replaced. Things—and eventually people—come to be regarded as interchangeable. Juanita's comment—"If Jimmy died, you could have another baby, and then you'd have two children again"—is an extreme example of this. To agree with this statement would have implied that I could be satisfied with any two children. Juanita and Jimmy, by implication, would be regarded as replaceable, not of particular importance or uniqueness to me or to them.

An Instinct to Resist

Although children may demand immediate replacement, attempting to avoid the pain of loss, they have a natural impulse to resist replacement. Anyone who has tried to remove the beloved blanket from the determined clutch of a three-year-old fist by offering another blanket realizes the strength of this instinct. Or try to give a child a different stuffed animal to sleep with, when his favorite dog has been temporarily misplaced, and discover that to the child, toys and blankets are not interchangeable. The popularity of Charles Schulz's Linus and his ever-present blanket testify to this truth.

Instinctively the child realizes that his "blankey" is not just any old piece of cloth. The meaning of the "blankey" includes the attachment he feels to it, its familiarity, its place in his daily routine. It includes the security of its remembered presence in the past and the reliability of its presence in the future. In some ways it is even an extension of himself. When the child loses a beloved "blankey," his grief includes, but is not limited to, grief over the loss of the security it represents and the emotional investment he has in it.

Unless adults understand this, their ways of dealing with a child's losses can weaken the child's natural instinct to resist a replacement. The child is already ambivalent, crying out for immediate replacement in order to avoid the pain of grief and yet instinctively resisting replacement. If the adults he loves and trusts hear only the cry for instant replacement, they may help him in his attempt to avoid the pain of grief. In so doing, the adult can cause the child to lose the sense of the uniqueness of each thing and person in his life; the child may learn to disregard his feelings and the emotional attachment he has to things, people, and places. The child may learn to ignore his feelings and discount the time, energy, and emotion he has invested in friends and possessions; if the child does not "learn" to ignore his feelings, he may try to protect them by refusing to care about things, people, and places.

Nothing is totally replaceable. Everything that matters to us is unique. A child may cry when the bouquet of dandelions he picked yesterday withers and is thrown away today. The withered dandelions cannot be replaced by a fresh bouquet picked today; part of their meaning is the fact that they are a part of the child's "yesterday" and were picked by him. When they are gone, so is his labor, his gift of love, and his "yesterday."

Denying Love

If we want our children to become loving, giving, involved adults, we must respect the attachments they have for people, places, and things. We need to reinforce the value of individual people, specific places, and special possessions. The fact that all our possessions and relationships are temporary, in the sense that we eventually lose all we hold dear, means that caring about people, valuing places, and treasuring things makes us vulnerable to suffering grief. As we respect the child's grief over his "small" losses, we reinforce the validity of his feelings and his caring. Discounting grief is also discounting the emotional investment the child had in what he lost; to care means that we run the risk of grief. To avoid grief altogether, we must also completely avoid love. The ability to grieve comes as we learn to love; denial of grief in the form of "it didn't really matter, anyway" is also a denial of love.

In the loss of Juanita's headband there were several fleeting instances of denial. First, we looked through her things again to make sure the headband wasn't there. Then, we had the impulse to go back and look for it at the recreation center. Last, we considered stopping and buying another pink headband to replace the lost one. When we decided not to go back and not to buy another one, we acknowledged the fact that the headband was really gone. At that point we moved from denial to other responses to the loss.

COMPLEX LOSSES

The loss of the headband was a simple loss. Therefore, denial was brief; the loss was relatively easy to accept and had minor emotional impact. Other losses are more complex. When we lose a loved one, a family pet, a prized possession, we suffer a host of other losses as well. These losses are of much greater emotional impact. In these, denial will reappear periodically as the extent of the loss is gradually realized and felt. The complex losses bring about grief that is more severe and lasts longer. This severe grief cannot be borne steadily. It is a heavy burden from which we must rest from time to time. The work of mourning is painful, takes time and energy, and requires periods of rest.

Change of Season

One example of a more complex loss, involving a variety of smaller losses, is the change of seasons. As we move from summer into fall, we experience a loss and may find ourselves grieving over summer. Included with this are many "small" losses: there is the loss of the season itself, with its warmth, long hours of daylight, green leaves and grass, growing gardens, lawns that need mowing; there is the loss of summer activities, such as swimming, tennis, golf, bicycle riding, and hiking; there is the loss of free time, unstructured by school and school-related activities; there may be the loss of the companionship of friends who are in different schools or different classes; there is the closing of the drive-in movie theaters and the corner ice cream stores. Each of these losses is part of the loss of summer; each, if felt and recognized as loss, can bring its own grief. Recognizing the different losses that are part of the loss of summer will take time, and there may be fresh grief as each new loss is discovered.

Many losses are also involved in the death of a friend or loved one. As a mother, I am many things to my children. I cook their meals, pack their school lunches, check their homework, accompany them on the piano when they sing or play their musical instruments, drive them to school and choir and swimming, attend their school events. I read their stories, help them write poems and songs, laugh at their jokes, play baseball and basketball and card games with them. When I am away from home, someone else takes over some of these activities, or some of them are suspended while I am gone. If I should die while my children depend on me for these things, they would lose me, what I contribute to their various activities, and probably lose some of their activities as well.

Each of these losses would bring its own grief. Wednesday would be a reminder that the three of us always go to church together for early Communion; swim days would be a reminder of our swimming together and my cheering for them; the piano would be a reminder of the times we have spent there together; games, clothes, pets, chemistry experiments, and quilt-making would all remind them of their loss. As each season of the year came for the first time after I was gone, it would bring out new losses, realized only in the context of that season. These all allow for the recurrence of denial and evoke new matters of grief that must be dealt with.

Categories of Loss

There are several categories of loss involved in the loss of a loved one or special possession. There is obviously the absence of the person or thing lost. There is the loss of routine, schedule, and security that depended on the one lost. Even the loss of a stuffed animal can change the routine of bedtime, naps, baths, and meals. When a person dies, such as Kathy's grandfather, the changes in routine and schedule are much more extensive and far-reaching. There is the loss of memories, secrets, and private jokes shared between the one who is left and the one who died; and the one left now has no one to share them with. There is the loss of plans and dreams that depended on the deceased person for their completion and fulfillment: projects that cannot be completed, trips that will not be taken, dreams that will never come true. There may also be a loss of a part of the bereaving individual because a relationship has ended; he will no longer see himself as he is reflected in the memories, thoughts, and eyes of the one who died.

When Peter Harris died, his son John was unwilling to go back to school. He was a good student in the third grade and had many friends there. He usually was out on the road early to meet the school bus, eager to be with his friends and on his way. After his father's funeral, however, it was different. Morning after morning he complained of a stomach ache and felt that he was "too sick" to go to school. His mother finally told him that she would go visit his room and his teacher with him, during one of the recess periods. She felt that his "sickness" indicated a reluctance to return to school, but she couldn't figure out the reason for it.

After they had visited the room and talked with his teacher, John blurted out, "I'm afraid the kids will laugh at me. I'm the only boy in the school without a daddy. The other kids will make fun of me."

A New Concept of Self

John found that his own concept of himself as a person changed with his father's death. Now he was "a boy without a daddy." This was new, strange, embarrassing, and frightening. He felt sure that the other children would see him this way too and make fun of him. The loss of his father changed him as a person in his own eyes, and he believed that the other children would also see this change; then his relationship with the other children in the school would change. In some ways, he felt like the "new boy" coming into the school in the middle of the year, when everyone else knew his way around, had friends, and had made a place for himself.

Janet solved the problem by pointing out to John two girls in his school whose mother was killed in an automobile accident during the summer. As John could see that they were accepted and liked by their classmates, he lost his own fear of his "differentness" and was willing to return to school.

With each of the myriad losses we encounter in the death of a loved one, we are given a chance to test its meaning in the pattern of our lives. As each new loss appears, denial may reappear. Yet denial is dropped gradually, through many opportunities to test the reality of the death and the meaning of the loss. As denial disappears, other reactions take over, and other coping mechanisms are used.

ANGER IN THE GRIEF PROCESS

A very common part of the grief process is anger. This may appear as soon as the denial is dropped or may even seem to overlap with it. In the loss of Juanita's headband, my next reaction after denial was exasperation, frustration, and anger. I was exasperated with Juanita for losing the headband and angry with myself for letting her lose it: "It was my fault for not thinking to have her take off the headband before she went swimming! . . . Maybe I should have gone back to look for it. . . . She's old enough to think of things like that for herself! . . . But I should have kept her from losing it! . . . Good grief! It's only a headband! Why can't she just forget about it?" Juanita's loss, and her grief over her loss made me feel very uncomfortable. I was helpless to undo the situation; this made me angry, with myself and then with her.

Out of Our Control

Loss brings with it a sense of helplessness and vulnerability. The situation has gotten out of our control. These feelings frequently result in anger. It is the difference between giving away twenty dollars and having the same twenty dollars stolen: Giving is under our control, and we tend to feel good about it; theft is out of our control, leaving us vulnerable and defenseless and often angry.

When we allow our children to experience a loss, we also experience the same feelings of helplessness and frustration. We cannot do anything about their loss or grief or discomfort; we cannot undo the loss, and by our choice, we are allowing them to experience the grief without instant replacement or distraction. Since this is at best an uncomfortable feeling, it is another reason why parents and other involved adults are slow to allow children to experience loss.

In the summer before her eighth birthday, Juanita participated in a tricounty swim meet for the first time. In the qualifying races she did extremely well and qualified for the finals in all three strokes she entered. The day of the finals was beautiful and sunny, and we were at the pool early to be ready for her events. We found a place on the deck, got a program for the day, and settled down to enjoy the meet. Juanita swam in her first event and placed third.

During the break between her first and second events, she went off to the restrooms to get a drink of water. While she was away, her next event was called. The PA system did not work in the restroom area, so Juanita didn't hear the call. When she returned to the bullpen, the alternate had already been put into Juanita's place. Juanita couldn't compete.

Of course, my little girl was crushed! She had really counted on going home with three ribbons; now she would have only two. She begged me to go to the officials and see if she could be reinstated. This was impossible, even though the race hadn't yet started: The rules stated that a swimmer who was absent from the bullpen when his event was called couldn't swim. Juanita cried, heartbroken. She refused to be comforted. I held her, sobbing, and said nothing. Then her coach approached. He lifted her onto his lap and let her cry on his shoulder. Finally he said, "Juanita, you still get to swim in two events. There's a little girl here who came as an alternate. Her only chance to swim is the race you missed. If you had swum in that race, she wouldn't have gotten to swim at all."

Juanita was comforted, and I later heard her explaining to some of her friends that she didn't mind missing the race so much because she knew it gave someone else a chance to swim who wouldn't have otherwise.

Personally I was furious! I was angry about the loudspeaker system that made it possible for Juanita not to hear her race called; I was angry with the officials for not taking into account the fact that Juanita couldn't hear; I was angry with myself for letting her leave the bullpen area; I was angry with her for leaving when she did.

Blame in Different Directions

Anger in the event of a loss can be part of our way of trying to get a handle on the situation, to get back in control. If we can figure out a reason for the loss, if we can blame something or someone for it, it seems easier to bear. This blame and anger tends to go in several different directions at once. We blame the others around us, children blame their parents or other adults, we blame the circumstances, and we blame ourselves.

Anger turned toward ourselves results in guilt: "I should have stopped this from happening!" Anger turned toward others results in blaming: "Why did you let this happen?" Both aspects of anger tend to appear together, so in dealing with a loss we may find both guilt and blaming. This is clearly illustrated in another "little death" situation, again involving Juanita.

Jimmy, Juanita, and I had gone shopping for valentines. In one store we found mugs and plates of bright, fire-engine red, decorated with white hearts. We decided to buy a plate and mug for a special friend. When we walked out of the store into the mall, I left Juanita sitting on a bench with the packages while I took Jimmy to the restroom. We returned to find Juanita in tears. The package with the plate and mug set had fallen off the bench as Juanita was rearranging our purchases, and the plate was chipped.

"Mommy, I'm so clumsy! You shouldn't have left me here with the packages! Now the plate's broken!" I held her for a while, then dried her tears. We looked for the tiny chip off the plate, and decided that we could mend it.

When we got home, Juanita rushed inside with the packages. Quickly she unpacked the mug, only to have it slip out of her hands and break into half a dozen pieces. She burst into tears again. "I'm so clumsy! I shouldn't touch anything, I'll just break it! It's my fault that the presents got broken!"

Later Juanita asked if I would go back and buy another plate and mug. "But don't take me along," she said, "because if I touch them, I'll just drop them and break them!" The loss of her present for our friend brought grief; she responded by blaming herself and me, and by feeling clumsy and good-for-nothing.

Whether it takes the form of blaming circumstances or others or the form of the guilt of self-blame, anger is a common response to loss. In a situation where we feel helpless and vulnerable, we ask, "Why did it happen?" and "Whose fault was it?" Especially in children, the sense of their littleness and impotence clashes with their feelings of omnipotence and their all-importance: Anything that happens to them must be their fault, yet they're too little and helpless to be held responsible, so someone else must be to blame. Therefore they simultaneously blame themselves and other people.

A Narrow Perspective

A child evaluates all happenings according to the effect they have on him. If his mother is sad, he wonders what he did wrong; if she is angry, he must be to blame; if she is happy, he takes the credit. Many things can be accomplished by his own thoughts and wishes: He goes where he decides, gets things by asking for them, wishes for things, and finds his wishes come true. As he believes that his thoughts and wishes are the way he gets the things he wants (Christmas presents, birthday gifts, special treats, even answers to prayers), he comes to feel also that his thoughts and wishes are more powerful than they really are.

Then, maybe "bad" things also happen because he thought about them or wished them. The sneaking suspicion that our dislike or anger could really harm someone, even if we never act on the feeling, lingers into adulthood; it is present and much more powerful in a child, particularly the child under nine. A small child faces a paradox between the realization of his smallness and weakness and his sense of importance and power. As the center of his universe, he is bound to feel guilt and responsibility over the loss of something important to him.

Moreover, not all the guilt children feel is false. Due to their short attention span and selective memories, they are often at fault in the loss of their possessions. This is pointed out to them frequently: a lost mitten, a broken toy, a forgotten book. In the death of a sibling, a parent, or a friend, they will feel blameworthy, as they have been blamed for other losses in the past. In fact, feelings of grief over a loss may trigger feelings of guilt associated with past grief. The feelings of grief are similar, whether the loss involves a favorite toy, a homework assignment, or a beloved person. In past losses they have felt guilty and have been to blame; grief over a loss through death tends to call up feelings of guilt.

Adults not infrequently deal with a child's losses by blaming the child. "Why didn't you remember your homework?" "Why did you forget your sweater at the baseball field?" "Can't you ever remember to pour the milk carefully?" "When will you learn to handle vases and cups carefully so they don't fall and break?" Imitating the behavior he has seen, the child may in turn blame others when he himself suffers a loss. "Adults are bigger, stronger, smarter; they can tie shoes, unstick stuck zippers, fix broken toys, glue broken cups, get kites out of trees, mend torn clothes. Why can't they also keep loss and grief away from the child? Why do they let him lose things, break things, suffer grief? Why can't daddy make the dog well? Why can't mommy bring back grandpa?" As the child is used to looking to the adults he loves and trusts to keep his world safe and secure, he is bound to turn to them with blame when loss disrupts his world and leaves him bereft.

Blaming God

For the child raised in the Christian faith who truly believes in the power and love of God, a loss may result in blaming Him. Even when the adults in his life are unable to do anything about a situation, God should be able. After all, Jesus healed the sick and raised the dead. The child has been told that Jesus still lives and that He is the same today as He was two thousand years ago. Why, then, does He let the child suffer the grief of loss? Why doesn't He intervene and make everything all right again?

So temporary anger is not abnormal in dealing with loss. But anger can also be constructive. If not carried to the extreme, self-blame may result in self-evaluation and the correcting of real shortcomings. Anger can also result in efforts to correct the situation, which may benefit both self and others. However, these are not automatic results of anger. The constructive use of the energy of anger must be learned. Part of the parents' role in helping children deal with grief is teaching them to use anger and guilt as tools, rather than being overwhelmed and defeated by these feelings.

Anger was involved in several ways in the "little death" situation with Juanita and the broken mug set. First, I refused to confirm Juanita's feelings of self-blame and guilt; instead, I held her and let her cry. When her grief over the loss of the presents eased, she herself came to the conclusion that she could be more careful and slow down to prevent accidents. After the anger, the tears, and the talking, we replaced the plate and mug. I took Juanita back to the mall. She carried the packages again. This time the presents were safely wrapped and delivered to our friend. Juanita asked me to glue together the broken plate and mug for her to keep, and I did.

Different Reactions

Jimmy's grief reactions are quite different from Juanita's.

43

Juanita expresses her grief in loud sobbing, retreating to her room, and not eating. Jimmy gets angry.

When John Hillis died, everyone but Jimmy cried and acted sad. His first response was matter-of-fact; "I'm glad he died. He used to shoot ducks, and I would pray for the ducks to get away. Now he can't shoot the ducks anymore." Under his calm, detached exterior, however, Jimmy was furious! He stomped around the house for days, slamming doors, throwing things, and taking offense at the slightest provocation. He was restless and always on the move. His little body was tense and rigid. He walked stiffly, wandered aimlessly around the house, and stopped eating.

Finally I had had enough! I followed him to his room one morning, opened the door he had just slammed shut, and walked in. I picked him up, stiff and unyielding, and set him on my lap. As he struggled to get away, I held him more tightly. "Put your arms around me," I ordered him "Hug me tightly. No, tighter! Tighter!" Finally his body wrapped around me in a big bear hug, and he held onto me with all his might. As he relaxed in my arms, the tears came.

For Jimmy, tears do not come easily. In part this is because he is a boy. Although we have tried to avoid the attitude that "big boys don't cry" in our home, it is strong in our society and has already influenced him. It is harder in our culture for boys and men to find release in tears than it is for girls and women.

Part of Jimmy's inability to cry easily is just the way he is. He is an intense, bright, rational, and verbal child. Ideas and facts are easier for him to deal with than emotions. It is easier and more natural for him to express grief by talking it out loudly and rapidly, acting it out in restless activity or wrestling matches, than to sit quietly and cry. I doubt that he feels grief much differently from others in the family, although signs of the anxious type of grief are more evident in him than the "sad" or depressed reaction. Tears are usually present, but they are often hidden deep inside, coming out only if he can pick a fight, misbehave and be yelled at, or find another reason for crying that is "legitimate" in his mind.

LOOKING FOR REASONS

During the past year Jimmy has been developing another mechanism for expressing his grief. He is moving into the stage of intellectual and rational exploration of the world. This means that Jimmy now looks for reasons and explanations for the loss he is grieving. He still shows a fair amount of anger, now usually in the form of finding someone or something to blame for the loss.

Just before Christmas, I took the children to the mall. Jimmy had his wallet and all his money with him; he was going to do some Christmas shopping and get something special for himself. We ended up at the pet store. After looking over the available pets and checking the contents of his wallet, Jimmy decided to buy himself a garter snake.

We took the snake home and fixed a vivarium for it. It was a calm, gregarious little animal. It enjoyed being held and petted and would twist itself into knots and sit quietly in the palm of your hand or ride around the house on Jimmy's neck. Jimmy named it "Fangs Stripe Dangerous" and played with it for hours.

For Christmas, Juanita received two chameleons and an African millipede to add to our menagerie. Because Jimmy was having so much fun with Fangs, Juanita bought him a second garter snake.

In early February we took a five-day trip to Chicago, asking a neighbor to feed the pets, water the plants, and pick up the mail while we were gone. As soon as we were home, Jimmy went downstairs to see how the pets were. The snakes and the chameleons were lively, but Millie the Millipede was curled up in a little black ball in one corner of the vivarium. Obviously there was something wrong. "Mommy, I think Millie's dead," he told me. "Come and see."

Sure enough, the millipede was still and looked unnatural. I poked at it with a finger, and it didn't stretch out the way it used to. I picked it up, and it lay limp and lifeless in my hand. "Yes, Jimmy, Millie's dead," I told him.

At first Jimmy didn't believe me. "Let's put it back in the vivarium. Maybe we should get an apple for Millie. Maybe Millie's just sick, not dead." But after touching the millipede himself, he was convinced of the truth.

Much to my dismay, Jimmy rushed upstairs to tell Juanita about her millipede. I didn't want to have to handle Juanita's grief right then! Sure enough, she plunged down the stairs and got her dead millipede. She and Jimmy handled it and looked it over. Then

Juanita took her dead pet, went upstairs, and locked herself into her room to cry. Jimmy followed me to the kitchen.

"Why did the millipede die? Did it get fed enough? I'll bet Judy didn't feed it; you know she didn't like it! We shouldn't take any more trips to Chicago, because then our pets will die! If we leave the pets with someone else, they don't take care of them!"

"Jimmy, I don't know why Millie died."

"Well, I bet Judy didn't feed Millie. Judy's afraid of millipedes."

"Honey, I don't think it was anyone's fault. Maybe Millie was old. We don't know how long millipedes live or how old it was when we got it. Maybe it got too cold in the house. I don't know what happened."

"When I looked at Millie, there was a crack in her shell. I bet that's the reason she died. Millipedes can't live with a crack in their shells."

Later on Jimmy came looking for me. "I think we need a new God," he told me.

"What do you mean?"

"Well, God let Millie die. He could have taken care of her, but He didn't. I think God hates me."

Jimmy was grieved. He expressed his grief by looking for reasons for the millipede's death until he found one that satisfied him—the crack in its shell. He also blamed us for taking a trip, Judy for not taking proper care of the pets, and God for letting it happen.

Juanita dealt with her grief in her typical fashion. She locked herself in her room to cry. Next, she demanded that I go right out to the mall and buy her another millipede. Then she found a flower pot full of dirt and gave Millie a funeral service and burial. She pestered me about another millipede for several days, until I called the pet store and found out that they wouldn't have any millipedes in stock until late spring. This information brought fresh tears of grief and anger from Juanita.

Not more than two weeks later, Fangs, Jimmy's favorite garter snake, died. Again he went through the endless questions about why it happened. Again I had no answers. Again he looked for reasons and for someone to blame.

"God doesn't care about me!" he exclaimed. "All He does is sit up there and kill our pets. First He let Millie die, and now my snake."

"Sometimes we don't know why God lets things happen the way they do. We can't always understand His reasons," I replied.

"Well, I can't see any point in His letting my snake die. Nothing good can come out of that. It can't help anyone. There's no reason why He should let my snake die!" Jimmy decided that God was to blame for letting the snake die, so he was angry with God; he didn't care who knew it, either. At the same time, he kept looking for a reason for death, a point that would make some sense out of his loss.

About a week later Jimmy reopened the question of his snake's death. "What reason could there be for God letting my snake die? It can't do any good. I'm not learning anything from it, and it isn't helping anyone."

"Well, why don't you ask God those questions?" I told him. "I don't know the answers. God knows what He's doing, and why. But if you're going to ask Him for answers, you'd better stick around so He can answer you."

"Why should I stick around? God can find me, no matter where I am."

"Yes, dear, but God isn't going to talk to you if you aren't listening. Ask Him your questions, but keep on listening until He gives you an answer."

Jimmy didn't seem to feel any guilt over his anger toward God, and this is unusual, even in a child. We tend to feel that we have no right to ask God questions, that questioning His ways is wrong. If we realize that we are angry with God as part of our grief, we may be shocked at ourselves and feel guilty for such presumptuousness.

Feeling Rejected

There are additional reasons for feeling anger and guilt while grieving for a loved one. We experience the absence of someone we love as rejection and abandonment. "If mommy really loved me, she wouldn't have died and gone away!" "Did grandpa die and leave me because he was angry with me?" "Did daddy die and go away because I was bad?" Even as adults we feel anger toward those we love who have died and left us; for children, the sense of abandonment can be much more acute, as the child's dependence on other people is usually much greater than the adult's. A parent-less child really would die if no one else came and took care of him, particularly the child under five. The parents are necessary to the child's physical life and well-being. The child also relies on physical presence and signs for reassurance that he is loved and accepted.

I recently sent Jimmy upstairs to take a bath and go to bed, since he was not getting along with anyone in the household. He stomped up the stairs and called for his dad. My husband, Jim, came down a little later with the message, "Jimmy said to tell you that he hates you." About five minutes later, Jimmy called me. He wanted me to hug him and hold him. He needed my physical presence and my hugs and kisses to reassure him that I still cared about him, still loved him, even though he was angry with me. He needed to know that my sending him upstairs was not a rejection of him.

When a parent or other loved one is dead, we no longer have that physical presence and hugs and kisses to reassure us that he or she loves us. Our feelings of rejection may be very strong and difficult to fight against in the absence of the one by whom we feel rejected. It is even more difficult for the child than for the adult.

Feeling Relief

Another feeling that is part of grief and that may also trigger guilt is the relief we often experience after a loss. No relationship is unmixed. Jimmy's first reaction to John Hillis's death illustrates this. He had admired and enjoyed John; he liked to be with John. He laughed at John's jokes and stories; no one could tell stories, play baseball, or catch fish like John Hillis. Still, there was one thing that Jimmy disliked about John, the fact that he would go duck hunting and kill ducks. Jimmy's concern over the ducks and his praying for them to get away now became unnecessary, as John Hillis was dead and couldn't go duck hunting anymore.

Children wish from time to time that their parents were dead or gone away so that they would not have to make their beds, practice the piano, comb their hair, or take baths. In fact, most children will express this wish at a time when they are angry and frustrated with their parents. From time to time they might also wish that their siblings would disappear: If a brother or sister were gone, they wouldn't have to share the basketball, the ice cream and cake, the hammock, or their parents' attention. If a parent or sibling dies, the child will have a sense of relief, an instinct that "Now I can play uninterrupted, now I can have his toys, now mommy won't spend so much time with her." This feeling usually appears late in the grief process, when some of the losses have been dealt with and the pain of the grief is beginning to ease. It may also be consciously present (and expressed, especially by children) even in the initial days after a loss.

Juanita was ill a lot one winter. During the last grading period in school, she was absent twenty-four of forty-three days. Part of the time was spent at home, some of it in the hospital. When she was mildly ill, I was willing to leave her at home alone part of the time; when she was hospitalized or very ill, I spent much of my time caring for her. This necessarily interrupted our usual family routine and schedule and left me with less time and energy for Jimmy than he thought he needed. Jimmy was incensed! "You're with Juanita all day long. She gets to stay home from school. You read to her and work with her. I want to stay home too. I want to be with you. You could teach me at home the way you teach her."

I cannot recall Jimmy's ever expressing the wish that Juanita would die, but when she got better and returned to school, his relief was evident. Now I would be able to make up to him the time that he "deserved" from me, which I had been spending with his sick sister. If she had died instead of getting well, there would still have been the relief of not having to share his mother's time and energy with a sick sister. Probably this relief would have been complicated with feelings of guilt for being "glad" that his sister had died.

If a pet dies, there is the relief of not having to feed it, bathe it, clean its cage, or in any way care for it anymore. If a favorite possession is broken or lost, there may also be relief at not having to look after it. Losses relieve us of responsibilities. In this relief from responsibility, there is a new freedom, a chance to start over again. It is one of the more positive sides that we put on our grief.

In some loss situations, the relief is much more prominent and may even outweigh the pain felt over the loss. The child who loses his place as an only child or the youngest child in the family through the birth of a sibling experiences a "little death"; yet, the privileges gained and the excitement and joy of a new baby may balance or even outweigh the sorrow and pain of the loss of his former position. In the "little death" of starting school for the first time, the gain of status as a school child, the gain of friends and companions, and the excitement of the new situation may all out-weigh the loss of free time, mother's attention, and home. In the "little deaths" experienced with the change of seasons, the gain and loss may balance each other out.

Relief may balance or outweigh pain. The death of a loved one who has endured a lingering, debilitating, humiliating, or painful illness can bring much relief; death of a family member or friend who has been the cause of much anxiety and distress can also result in great relief; even suicide, if it happens after years of concern and fear that it might occur, can bring with it a sense of relief.

Losses, and the grief we experience because of them, strip us and cleanse us. They can leave us stronger and more ready to go on to new experiences, new responsibilities, new joys, and new loves. They can leave us freer than we were, less restricted in our choices and the possibilities for our lives. The way in which we handle the grief process and accomplish the painful and difficult task of mourning determines whether this will be the outcome of our grief.

3 // THE TASK OF MOURNING

GRIEF AND MOURNING go together, like pain and suffering. The words *grief* and *mourning* are often used interchangeably, but there is a difference between them. They represent two facets of the same experience.

Grief is the complex of feelings experienced as the result of a loss, the feelings described in chapter 2. Grief is observed in a variety of physical symptoms and behavior that express the feelings. Mourning, in my usage, denotes the emotional and psychological work that is performed by a person during the grief process.

The task of mourning includes the following:

—Identifying the extent of the loss;

—Testing the reality and meaning of the total loss;

—Severing emotional ties with the person or object that has been lost;

—Redefining personal identity in the absence of that which was lost;

—Incorporating aspects of that which was lost into the life of the bereaved;

—Completing a memory of the person or object lost;

—Recovering the emotional energy that was invested in the thing lost, and freeing that energy for investment in new relationships or activities.

The initial result of a loss, particularly a severe one, is a diminished person—one who has lost a part of his identity and self-respect, who is fearful of love, and who avoids emotional involvement because of the risk of further loss and pain. In accomplishing the work of mourning, this same severe loss may result in a growing person—one who is stronger, freer, and ready to face new challenges, new responsibilities, new joys, and new loves. The difficult and painful work of mourning, if undertaken and carried through, has enormous potential for good in our lives. Mourning can be distorted, incomplete, or deferred—but only with the result of leaving long-term scars in the emotions and personality of the bereaved.

THE BENEFITS OF MOURNING

An episode in C. S. Lewis's book, *The Voyage of the Dawn Treader,* illustrates the positive aspects of the grief process and the task of mourning. Eustace Clarence Scrubb is a hateful, totally rational, unfeeling, logical, greedy, arrogant boy. (Lewis says, "He almost deserved the name"!) On an island in the land his cousins have discovered, Eustace becomes a dragon. He falls asleep in a dragon's cave, on the dragon's hoard of stolen treasure, thinking "greedy, dragonish thoughts." The dragon is dead; when Eustace awakes, the dragon's skin has become his own. After a series of adventures as a dragon, Eustace changes. The boy inside the dragon skin has become compassionate and caring, sorry for his past attitudes and actions.

One night—whether waking or dreaming, Eustace isn't sure—he is visited by Aslan, the Great Lion of Narnia. Eustace is terribly afraid. Fearful, nervous, shaking, Eustace follows the lion up a mountain to a clear mountain pool. There he longs to bathe. The lion speaks, either aloud or in Eustace's mind. He tells Eustace that he must undress before he may bathe. At first Eustace is puzzled. He isn't dressed; how can he undress? Then he understands. He scratches vigorously at his scales and succeeds in shedding his dragon skin. Underneath the first skin is another!

Eustace sheds several skins, finally feeling hopeless. How many skins does he have to shed before he is "undressed" and may bathe? Again the lion speaks: "Let me do it for you." Eustace, now desperate but still frightened, agrees. The lion's claws tear deep into his skin as if they are going "straight to the heart." It is dreadfully painful. In the end, however, Eustace the boy is free of the dragon's skin. He bathes in the deliciously cool water, and the lion dresses him in new clothes.

We are Eustace, clothed in skins more or less like a dragon's.

Loss strips us. It leaves us "undressed"—helpless, vulnerable, and emotionally naked. Through the period of grief, the work of mourning is accomplished; we heal. At the end, we are ready for "new clothes"—an alteration in our identity, a chance to explore new opportunities, to grow in new directions, to enter new relationships.

I believe that each of us is like Eustace, a "real" person trapped under layers and layers of skins. To use another analogy, each of us is like a block of marble. To the casual observer, a block of marble is just stone. A sculptor, however, can see within the marble a beautiful, unique sculpture, for which this particular block of marble is especially suited. It takes time and work as the sculptor chips away the marble bit by bit to uncover the object of beauty that his eyes alone can see. For us to become who we really are, we must be stripped of the "chunks of marble" that hide our true identity. Each "little death" is part of the sculpting process. Each experience of loss and grief frees us to some degree and gives us new choices. We may choose again who we will be; we may choose to let go of the stone that hides the real person, the person God has made us to be.

Faced With a Choice

A feeling of relief, discussed in chapter 2, comes in realizing the new freedom that is ours as a consequence of our loss. At that point we are faced with a choice of what to do with our new freedom. We may use it to explore new avenues of growth; on the other hand, we may try to "go back" to where we were before the loss, avoiding our freedom as too frightening and risky.

When Juanita missed her opportunity to swim an event in the tricounty meet, her loss was a "little death." As a result of this "little death," she became a slightly different person. She had a new feeling of compassion for the children who did not qualify to swim in the finals. She had a new acceptance of her own responsibility for her events, to remain where she belonged and be in the bullpen when her events were called. She also had a new respect and affection for her swim coach. These results were not automatic; they were the outcome of her own real—though probably unconscious—choices. She could have chosen to sit out the rest of the meet, angry and sorry for herself, refusing to swim her other event. She could have refused her coach's offer of comfort and thus cut herself off from his affection and understanding. She could have denied any responsibility for herself, insisting on blaming me, the coach, the officials of the meet, and the PA system.

INTANGIBLE LOSSES

In the same way that the feeling of relief is usually an endpoint in the grief process, so the choices of new directions and new growth are also generally among the final tasks of mourning. The work of mourning begins in testing the reality of the loss and discovering its extent and meaning in our own lives. Most losses are more complex than they at first appear. The loss of a "tangible"—that is, something or someone we can see, hear, taste, touch, and feel—generally makes itself felt in terms of the intangible losses we suffer in consequence. Intangible losses are often harder to recognize; they include the routine, schedule, plans, hopes, dreams, memories, insight, understanding, acceptance, and sharing that are ours only in relationship to the person or object that is lost.

Even in our "little deaths" we suffer intangible losses. Jimmy misplaced a wallet with ten dollars in it. The wallet itself and the money were the tangible parts of his loss. The intangible losses involved the meaning to him of the wallet and the money. The wallet was a present, a keepsake from a trip Jim and I had taken; it included memories for Jimmy of the week he had spent with friends and grandparents. The ten dollars represented weeks of allowance and hours of work, including mowing the lawn, doing dishes, taking out the garbage, and other chores; it also represented dreams and plans for the future, the things he could have bought with it. The loss even had an impact on the way Jimmy saw himself: With ten dollars he was "rich"; when it was gone, he was "poor." The intangible losses Jimmy suffered when he lost his wallet were things I would not have thought of, had I not been thinking about grief and mourning and closely analyzing losses. You can imagine the great rejoicing when the wallet and the money turned up several months later!

The child of two or three who loses his "blankey" also suffers a number of intangible losses. He has lost an extension of himself; he has lost security and continuity in his life; he has lost part of his bedtime and naptime routine. The "blankey" may be one of the strongest emotional attachments he has; its loss may be one of his earliest exposures to grief and mourning.

Testing Reality

To a large degree, testing the reality of a loss means discovering the intangible losses we have suffered. The meaning of a loss in our own lives is usually translated into the intangibles: Grandma's special appreciation of our jokes, dad's leadership in our hiking and exploring, the way the dog barks and jumps to welcome us when we come home, the plans and dreams we have for ways of getting the most enjoyment out of an ice cream cone, a bar of chocolate, or the ten dollars we have saved.

However, before we are able to test its meaning, we must accept the fact that we have really suffered a loss. When Juanita lost her headband, she had to check her possessions to make sure it wasn't there; she had to ask me to return and look for it; she had to hear me refuse to stop and replace it. After these steps, she was sure the headband was really gone.

When Millie the Millipede died, both Juanita and Jimmy had to take her out of the vivarium, handle her, pet her, try to feed her, feel the limpness of her body, find her unresponsive to handling and stroking. Then they were able to realize that Millie was really dead. Juanita also had to have me call a number of pet stores, and find out that none would have African millipedes in stock for several months, before she could begin dealing with the loss of her pet.

Part of realizing a loss comes only when we can "see for ourselves." We are physical beings; what we can see, hear, touch, taste, and feel is more real to us than what we learn only by hearing. The child who is allowed to see for himself that the "blankey" is gone, to go out to the doghouse and find it empty, to call grandma's number on the telephone or go to her house and find her not there, will have a more complete realization of the fact of his loss than one who does not have these physical confirmations.

As the child is allowed to test the reality of his loss by "seeing for himself," its meaning begins to become apparent. This is his discovery of the intangible aspects of his loss. Our intangible losses take time to realize, because these losses are more personal and more private than the sensory ones. Dreams, plans, and ideas that exist in the seclusion of our own minds, shared with no one, may be the intangibles we grieve. A parent or other "outsider" may not understand the extent of the child's grief and his need to mourn, unless he has some idea of the various intangible losses included with the tangible ones.

Several categories help us define the various intangible losses. These include:

—The loss of shared memories and a part of our own past;

—The loss of daily routine and schedule;

—The loss of a part of ourselves, or the way we see ourselves;

—The loss of the way we see and understand another person, particularly the person we have lost;

—For a child, the loss of the sense of omnipotence and omniscience of parents;

—The loss of the way we see and understand God.

These kinds of intangible losses generally make up the meaning of a loss in our lives. As we discover them, accept them, mourn them, let them go, and find ourselves again, we accomplish the task of mourning.

The Importance of Memories

We generally think of memories as the province of "old folks." They are the ones who sit around and reminisce about the old days and old ways. Yet a child's memories are as important to him as anyone else's. Our memories are our own personal history; they are our past, the foundation of our present, the roots of who we will become.

From time to time my children will spring a "remember when" question on me. Sometimes I am at a total loss; the incident that is so vivid in the child's memory made no impression on me. Sometimes the two of them share memories that I don't share. The memory is brighter, more joyful, more real when they share it with each other; their eyes sparkle, and they talk with excitement and animation, interrupting each other to add details and complete the picture or the story. For a brief moment, the two of them are lost, gone off together into their private, shared past. There is a sense of sadness when a treasured memory of theirs is not shared by anyone else in the family; the sparkling moment falls flat, and something precious is lost.

Our slide collection and the children's picture scrapbooks hold a wealth of memories of our shared past. These memories are their past, the basis of their future. The loss of these objects would put some of those memories out of reach and mean the loss of a part of their lives. Shared or private memories may be a significant part of the loss a child feels in losing favorite possessions, changing schools, moving to another house, or losing a friend or loved one through death, divorce, or distance.

Our memories and our past are also involved in the loss of landmarks and places important to us. Visiting an old home, to find it has been repainted and the yard landscaped differently, is this kind of loss. Going to visit an old school, to find it gone— demolished and replaced by a shopping center—is another instance. To find that the favorite neighborhood McDonald's has given way to new office buildings, that the empty lot of many Saturday explorations is now the site of an apartment building, that the cow pasture where you caught crickets and grasshoppers is now the site of a new housing development—all involve the loss of memories and a part of your own personal past.

A Change of Routine

Another intangible loss lies in a daily or weekly routine and schedule. By the age of five or six, a child has become a creature of habit. His schedule and his daily routine are very important to him The future is beginning to have meaning to him in terms of the things he is planning to do, the routines and habits that will be continued. "But you promised!" is a wail of grief and anger when something comes along to interrupt a child's plans. Loss of routine, familiar rituals, or a customary schedule represent the loss of a certain type of security and of a part of the future. These are part of the loss the child encounters when a new baby is born into the family, when friends or relatives move away, when the family moves, or when the child changes schools.

Even normal changes in schedule that come as a child grows up involve a certain loss in routine: Starting school, changing grades, going from fall to winter, giving up a doll or toy to sleep with, sleeping without a night light, or coming to the end of the swimming season.

When John Hillis died, part of Jimmy's loss lay in things he had counted on doing with John. John had promised to take Jimmy fishing, to come to his birthday party, to play baseball, to wrestle with him. Jimmy "saved" stories and jokes to share with John. When John died, Jimmy lost these things.

A Sense of Identity

One of the most personal and private intangible losses is the sense of one's own identity that comes with the loss of something or someone we love. Jimmy's need to readjust his ideas of himself from a "rich" little boy to a "poor" little boy when he lost his wallet is an example.

Our sense of identity is complex, fragile, and precious. It is determined by the physical body and its abilities, our mental capabilities, our reactions to other people and their reactions to us, our special skills and talents, the things we are able to do, and the things we are asked to do. Our personal sense of who we are is shaped by the reflection of ourselves we see when we look at those around us; who we are in our own estimation is largely determined by who other people think we are. This is particularly important for a child.

As the infant is learning about himself and his body, the difference between himself and others, and the differences between people and things, his learning is shaped by what others tell him. He learns to recognize the parts of his body and to know them as his own through his interactions with other people. When the baby first grabs his feet and tries to suck on his toes, someone says, "Oh, look! Baby found his feet!" We play games with a baby—Pat-a-Cake, This-Little-Piggy, Peekaboo—using parts of his body and teaching him to use them himself. We teach him names for the different parts of his body, telling him at the same time that they belong to him. We distinguish between the things that are his and those that belong to others. He learns to say "Mine!" about his body and his toys.

We applaud and emphasize a baby's mastery of the skills of sitting, standing, crawling, and walking. We also warn him of danger to himself, telling him "No!" or "Hot!" The child's sense of accomplishment in gaining skills and mastery over his body and his world is a reflection of the excitement and pride those around him show as he learns new skills. He hears his parents and others discuss his development: "Johnny got his first tooth! Sally sat up by herself today! Jenny is almost toilet trained!" The pride and joy of the parents and grandparents in the child's development and accomplishments is reflected in the child's sense of well-being and all-rightness.

If there is a question in the parents' minds about the child's development—if they feel that he is slow, uncoordinated, or unresponsive—this doubt also becomes a part of the child's feelings about himself. A child will believe that he is "smart," "dumb," "cute," "strong," "slow," "clumsy," "careful," or "sloppy" if he hears himself described that way often enough. He believes what others say about him, and their ideas are incorporated into his sense of identity. Jimmy can come crying into the house, devastated because "Juanita said I was dumb!"—or he can come home walking on air, his eyes shining, when "Mr. Charles asked me to sing the solo part in choir, and he said I did a good job!" or "Everyone at the potluck liked my brownies and complimented me on them!"

Often a child is five or six before he even begins to question the statements made about him by friends, teachers, playmates, or neighbors. As his sense of his own identity becomes stronger and more secure, he will start to evaluate the comments of others and accept or reject them according to his own knowledge of himself. Even in this process, however, he will go to an adult he knows and trusts, or to an older child whom he admires, to ask, "Am I dumb? Joe said I was," or "Mommy, do you think that Brad really can run faster than I can? He said he could." Of course, this testing is not restricted to children. We adults also ask those we love and trust to help us know who we are. We also test the statements made about us by others, by asking people who know us and love us to evaluate the statements with us.

When we lose someone who is close enough to us to tell us who we are, we also lose a part of ourselves. We lose that person's judgment of our feelings about ourselves, his perspective on what we do and what others say about us. We lose the security we have in our own evaluation of ourselves that is provided by that person's agreement and support. This loss may not be the death of the individual; it may be the severing of the relationship because of a change in schedules, a move, a job change, a change of schools, or new friendships or responsibilities that make this person unavailable to us.

Our sense of identity may vary from day to day. The way we feel about ourselves can change unpredictably, depending on the weather, our state of health, the amount of sleep we have had, our energy level, tensions in the family, and other factors. We learn to check out the way we feel about ourselves with people we can trust, in order to accommodate the things that influence our feelings about ourselves without really changing our identity.

Jimmy has been subject to fairly strong feelings of depression off and on for a couple of years. When he is "down," he sees himself as good for nothing, unable to do anything right. But he learned by age eight that the way he feels about himself when he is "down" isn't necessarily who he is. He is beginning to come to Jim and me when he is depressed, to share the way he feels about himself, and to allow us to tell him who he is. His feelings of depression distort his judgment; when he is depressed, he even looks different to himself in the mirror. As Jimmy is learning that there is a difference between "I feel as if I'm no good" and "I'm no good," he uses his father and me to help him know who he is. Loss of either of us would include, for Jimmy, loss of this help is knowing who he is, especially at times when negative feelings cloud his judgment.

As a child grows, he becomes more selective in the people he allows to tell him who he is. A two-or-three-year-old tends to see all adults as authorities on all topics. By the age of five or six, the child has begun to discriminate. Miss Fletcher, the first-grade teacher, has authority because of her position that begins to rival the authority of the parents. A minister or Sunday school teacher becomes an authority about God, the Bible, and right and wrong behavior. At the age of nine or ten, friends become extremely important; what they say about a child's looks, dress, behavior, intelligence, knowledge, and skills carries a great deal of weight. The good opinion of friends can be even more important to the child at this age than the good opinion of parents. We come to count on certain friends and loved ones to be the authorities in different areas of our lives. Praise from grandpa for throwing or hitting a baseball well becomes more important than mother's comments on the way we play ball. If Rosalie compliments Juanita on her table manners, it carries far more weight than the same compliment coming from grandma. Doug's comments about

Jimmy's singing mean much more to Jimmy than what Juanita or his father says about his singing.

As a child learns to differentiate between people, he comes to appreciate the uniqueness of each individual. His relationships with people are also different, depending on the differences he sees between them. His friends and loved ones become less and less interchangeable in his life. The child also "becomes" a slightly different person in his different relationships; with different people he reveals aspects of his personality that correspond to or complement their personalities; he develops aspects of himself that are part of a special relationship. Juanita has friends with whom she is giggly and silly, friends with whom she talks about books and ideas, friends with whom she plays dolls. Sometimes I can tell which friend she has been with, just by the way she acts when she comes home. As the child develops an ability to see people as individuals, and to form relationships with others based on the uniqueness of each person, his loss of a loved one will also involve the special place that person had in his life. He will lose the self he has "become" in that relationship.

Very Special People

From time to time, very special people enter our lives. They seem to see us in a totally different light from others who know us. They can see talents, abilities, potential, and beauty in us that no one else sees. One word for these people is *mentor*. A mentor is a trusted counselor or guide. He or she helps us, to an unusual degree, to know who we are and who we can be. He or she can excite and challenge us to develop special talents and abilities. The mentor may also exhibit a personality or a way of life that motivates us to copy it.

These mentor relationships are usually so strong that they mark turning points in our lives. They leave us feeling good about ourselves, more confident of who we are, with a stronger sense of purpose and direction. A mentor may be the fifth-grade teacher who challenged me to become a straight-A student, or the eighth-grade teacher who encouraged me to write; he may be the choir director who noticed Jimmy's unusual capability for understanding and learning music; she may be the band director who challenged a fifth-grader to become an outstanding French horn player; she may be the nurse whose kindness and understanding comforted a frightened little girl and gave birth to the determination, "That's what I want to be when I grow up!"

The loss of a mentor is a "little death." However, in many instances the relationship with a mentor is short-term and is expected to end. In these instances, the normal progress of the relationship is such that the grief may go unnoticed, and the work of mourning proceeds naturally and unconsciously. If the mentor relationship is ended abruptly, before the child is ready to let the mentor go, his loss will involve his own identity to a great degree. Mourning the loss of the mentor means that the child must come to a new understanding of who he is.

Other Losses in Self-Image

There are other losses in which the child's personal identity and self-image play a major part. Because we are physical beings, the person we see in the mirror—the body that responds to our desire to smile, walk, or run—is a large part of who we are. Loss of a part of our body is a loss of part of ourselves. Even the "hidden" parts of our body, such as the tonsils or appendix, count. "Small" things like a haircut, new glasses, or different clothes change the way we look and the way we see ourselves. The loss of an arm or a leg, a scar, losing our hair (due to illness or certain types of medication), and temporary or permanent paralysis have a profound effect on self-image. Polio, a sprained ankle, poison ivy, hives, a broken arm, noticeable weight loss or gain, acne, and similar changes in the body influence our self-image. This is true even if the loss or change is one we have looked forward to and anticipated. If the change comes without preparation and anticipation, it may be traumatic and involve real grief. Body changes at puberty, including the change in voice for boys and beginning of menstruation for girls, may be welcomed as a sign of maturity and also grieved as a loss of childhood. Some personal identity is lost when such a person begins to see himself or herself as a teen-ager instead of a child.

The Fall From Omnipotence

Just as knowing who we are is a part of our security in life, so knowing who others are—how they are likely to act, what they will say and do—is a part. When we find that people are not who we thought they were, we may suffer a loss. A growing awareness of parents as limited and human instead of omnipotent and godlike brings a sense of loss. Much of a child's security is bound up in his sense of the strength, wisdom, rightness, and goodness of his parents. When a child is bereft by a loss that shakes his world, he is also faced with the fact that his parents are not strong enough, big enough, or wise enough to prevent this loss, to forestall grief. If, in addition, the child sees his parents grieve, he becomes aware of their vulnerability as well. They cannot do "anything," fight "anyone"; they are no longer automatically the "strongest," "fastest," "wisest," or "best." This makes it necessary for a child to reevaluate his view of his parents and his dependence on them for his security.

Children usually come to realize their parents' limitations and faults gradually and are able to cope with the loss little by little. Even so, this loss brings grief. The realization that his parents are not the gods that he imagined them to be requires the child to rethink his view of the world, his place in it, and the part his parents play. When the loss of his ideas of his parents compounds the loss of a loved one, a beloved pet, a home, or a part of his body, the child's grief will be more severe and prolonged.

Understanding About God

The last and most crucial intangible loss any of us, child or adult, has to face is the loss of our ideas about God and our understanding of Him. It isn't a far step from learning to believe in God as all-wise, all powerful, and all-good to questioning His power, wisdom, and goodness when things happen that destroy our world. Particularly in a Christian home—where one is taught that God is bigger, stronger, wiser, and more loving than even the parents or grandparents—a child's belief in God is tested when he suffers loss and experiences grief. He is forced to come to terms with a belief in a wise, loving, all-powerful God on the one hand and a world in which sickness, death, and pain are allowed to exist on the other hand.

This testing is a lifelong process. Because we are finite and God is infinite, we are never able to understand Him completely. Each time we come to an understanding of Him that satisfies us, He eventually pushes us to give up that understanding and to learn to

63

know more of who He is. Jimmy began verbalizing his own dealing with this question at a very young age. I believe that this is a common concern for children, even pre-schoolers, although it may be unconscious or nonverbal. Children vary widely in their need and ability to put feelings into words, and the fact that a child has not talked about this concern does not mean he has not felt it.

When a child's belief in the omnipotence of his parents or the omnipotence and love of God is threatened, his security is threatened. These intangible losses of what we thought and believed about others bring grief. Even if these losses are not verbalized or consciously identified, they may contribute significantly to the grief of a child faced with a major crisis.

The intangible loss resulting from finding out that someone we loved wasn't everything we thought he was may come long after the person has gone. A child may learn new facts about a friend or loved one long after that person's death, divorce, or distancing. Even if the new facts are positive, the child experiences a loss of his own idea of who the person was. If what he learns is negative—that his father was an alcoholic, that his mother beat him as an infant, or that his friend was in trouble with the police—the new grief may be even more severe than the original grief. Even a seemingly small thing, such as the information that grandma didn't know how to read and write, can alter the mental picture of grandma sufficiently to cause grief as the child realizes she wasn't everything he had thought.

Discovering Losses Gradually

Many intangible losses are not discovered immediately. Some may not appear until years after the child has lost the person he loved. It takes time to identify, test, and accept all the losses involved. For this reason it is impossible to predict accurately the amount of time needed for a child to complete his mourning in a specific loss situation. The appearance of fresh grief after we thought a child had finished mourning does not necessarily mean that the mourning process was inadequate or abnormal; it may mean only that a new facet of the loss has been discovered and must also be mourned.

THE BEHAVIOR OF MOURNING

In the initial period of mourning, an individual, whether child or adult, may tend to withdraw from normal patterns of living. Juanita runs to her room, locks the door, throws herself on her bed, and covers her head with a pillow. This is a vivid picture of withdrawal. On the other hand, Jimmy stalks around the house, usually staying near the family but not really a part of it. He too may go to his room, but he will return almost immediately and wander back and forth between his room and the kitchen or living room, wherever the rest of the family can be found. Other children do not appear to withdraw at all, but demand constant companionship and activity; even in this activity and involvement, however, there is withdrawal in the sense that the patterns and routines of living are abandoned and replaced.

The time of withdrawal coincides with the first testing of the reality of the loss. In the initial mourning period, the pain of grief is so sharp and so fresh that the child withdraws from the routine and suspends his usual activities as a form of emotional protection. He unconsciously avoids new experiences, new friends, and new relationships; he is reluctant to invest in anything and anyone emotionally, afraid of more loss and pain. Depending on whether the signs of depression or anxiety are more prominent, the child may withdraw physically, becoming less active and spending more time alone, or he may withdraw by replacing familiar routines and schedules with different, busy, and sometimes aimless activity.

Partial Withdrawal

Withdrawal is rarely complete. Juanita will retreat to her room, but she doesn't leave the house. Jimmy wanders around, but he is always within sight or sound of the rest of the family. The grieving child seeks the security and protection of old friends, old familiar places, and old habits; however, he soon finds that these things are not what they used to be. His favorite books seem to have lost their appeal; favorite foods are suddenly unappetizing; his own special, private retreat becomes foreign and unwelcoming.

The impact of a severe loss changes everything, even things that seem not to be related to it. The child finds it necessary to remove himself from normal, routine activities and places until he is able to identify the differences introduced into the secure patterns of life by the loss. The child retains a hold on the familiar habits that represent security, but it is a loose grip, keeping these things at a distance while he learns all over what is normal, dependable, and secure. Withdrawal is a buffer, less intense and unconscious than denial, but still a form of shielding the emotions from the full impact of loss and grief.

A frenzied, compulsive involvement in new activities, relationships, and interests may also be a form of withdrawal. Some children attempt to escape the pain of grief by breaking completely with the past, the normal, and the expected. A child may keep himself so busy and become so physically exhausted that no time or energy is left over for mourning. However, a totally new event, unrelated to what was lost, can also be a sharp reminder of loss. The child may think, "I can't wait to tell grandpa," only to remember that grandpa is dead and can no longer share the child's joy, wonder, amusement, or indignation over the new situation. A child encountering such pain in a new situation may react by switching to the other form of withdrawal. Periods of intense activity may alternate with periods of quiet in the grieving child.

Another form of withdrawal is the regression of the child to earlier forms of coping with stress. To escape the pain of his present life, he retreats to a younger self. He seeks the security and continuity of his earlier world. A child may begin sucking his thumb again, wetting the bed, sleeping with a stuffed animal or blanket, or asking for a night light. This regression is natural, normal, and nearly inevitable. It tends to resolve itself spontaneously, with the child voluntarily returning to his older, more mature self. A night light may be particularly significant: at night we are tired and our defenses are down; we are more likely to be aware of our fears and insecurities; the dark itself may be seen as a powerful, threatening enemy.

Severing Emotional Ties

The major work of mourning is severing the emotional ties to the person or object lost. This involves reestablishing a personal identity without that which was lost, building a memory of it, and forming new patterns and routines of normal life in the absence of it. During the time of withdrawal, the emotional ties to the lost person or thing begin to weaken. As the child suspends his normal activities and routine for a while, the place occupied in his life by that which he lost begins to lose its hold. The child begins to adopt new patterns which are no longer dependent on the lost. His self-image and personal identity begin to adapt to the fact of the loss. He tests his new routines and new identity as he continues to explore the extent of the loss. He also forms a memory of what he lost. Much of this work takes place naturally and normally, on an unconscious level.

Severing emotional ties in the mentor relationship is a short-term process. There is an initial period of intense attachment, in which the child spends much time with the mentor; his time away from the mentor is occupied by thinking and talking about him. The child may adopt the habits and mannerisms, copy his likes and dislikes, and "become" a carbon copy of the mentor. In the early period of mourning, the child may also spend a lot of time thinking and talking about the person he has lost and may consciously or unconsciously copy his behavior and attitudes. He may also try to act in a way that he believes would please the person he has lost. An identification may be negative as well as positive, with the child becoming the opposite of the person he has lost, behaving in ways that are as different as possible from him.

Eventually the child comes to a point where he no longer needs the mentor as intensely. He begins breaking the ties slowly, spending less time with him, and talking and thinking about him less often. He begins to make decisions on his own, without discussing them with his mentor, and refers less often to what his mentor would think, say, or do in a situation. He also copies the mentor less faithfully in matters of dress, mannerisms, habits of speech, and likes and dislikes.

As the mourning period progresses, the grieving child begins to let go of the person he has lost. He thinks of him less, talks about him less, and is less intense in his imitation. He begins to speak, act, and think with less reference to what "dad would do," "mom would say," "Joe would think." Negative identifications tend to be stronger than positive ones, and the child who has "become" the opposite of the person may continue these contradictory habits and attitudes much longer than the child who has made a positive identification.

Ready to "Let Go"

After a time, the child has absorbed into his personality those things about his mentor that are truly a part of him. He adapts habits, thinking, and action he has learned from his mentor to his own personality and individuality. He also has a picture of the mentor and an appreciation of him that is now a part of memory. When the "break" with the mentor is complete, the child is left with a positive, happy, affectionate memory that will always be a part of his life. So too with the loss of a person the child loves and admires, there comes a time when the child is ready to "let go." He stops waiting for the person to return and becomes comfortable in living with the memory. At this point the child is also usually ready to take a more realistic view of the lost person. Instead of seeing him in black and white, he is able to admit that he was a combination of virtues and faults. He can admit shortcomings in one he has fiercely admired and defended; he is able to concede that there are good points about someone he has violently disliked.

The break with the mentor—the "letting go" of the person the child has lost—is not a forgetting or an obliteration of all his feelings. There may actually be a deeper affection and love, a greater appreciation and understanding of the individual. However, the time and energy involved in the relationship begin to decrease. The intensity of the emotional involvement abates, and the child has emotional energy free to turn in new directions.

The process of assimilating aspects of the personality of the lost one and assembling a memory has a very individual timetable. This timetable is influenced by the child's age, the relationship to the person who was lost, the manner of loss, and the child's personality and individual style of mourning.

Upon completion of the mourning process, the child has become a new person. He has a new pattern of life, without that lost thing. He has recovered his self-image and identity and no longer depends on the lost relationship. He has a memory of the person or object that will always be a part of him. And he has emotional energy that is now free to be invested in new loves, new relationships, new activities, and new avenues of personal growth.

4 FUNERALS ARE FOR THE LIVING

WHEN JOHN HILLIS DIED, Jim, Juanita, Jimmy, and I all attended the funeral. John had been a friend of the whole family. Jimmy was five and Juanita was seven.

We filed past the open casket, then took our seats in the pew just behind John's wife and children. When the time came to sing "Jesus, Lover of My Soul," Juanita leaned over and whispered, "Mommy, that was John's favorite hymn!" Other favorite songs were played and sung. We listened to the minister review John's life: He had been very handy with his tools and loved fixing things for himself and for others; John had been a great practical joker; he had been a good leader for young people, who loved his sense of humor, his ability in sports, his knowledge of the outdoors; he had spent much time visiting and cheering others who had the same illness he did; he had loved the outdoors and often went hunting or fishing with his friends. The picture painted of John was warm, real, and alive, and we found ourselves smiling even as we shared the tissue box.

After the service, we joined the funeral procession to the cemetery for the graveside service. We crowded around the gaping hole in the ground, under the canopy, with John's other close friends and family. We shared in a brief service. We embraced John's wife and children, then left the cemetery and John's casket and returned to the church for a meal.

The meal was a splendid potluck. John would have loved it! People talked, laughed, cried. We remembered John, laughed over some of his outrageous practical jokes, shared stories of the kindness he had shown to us, and missed him. We shared his memory with other people who had also known and loved him, people we knew well and some we knew scarcely at all. We were drawn together with his other friends by the fact that we had all known John and loved him.

When we left the church after the meal, there was a sense of completion. Somehow, we knew John better now than we had known him before. We were sad about his death, but happy about the life he had lived and proud to have been his friends.

THE END OF A SENTENCE

A funeral is a punctuation mark; like the period at the end of the sentence, it signals a full stop. Death is an ending; the family circle, the circle of friends, is broken when one member dies. It takes time before the break can be repaired and a new circle formed. The funeral underlines this ending. With ceremony and ritual it emphasizes the fact of death and loss, making it real. It makes us stop and think. It gives us time to let the ending of our way of life sink in.

Personal in Style

Funerals are as different in style as the people who plan them and take part in them. A funeral is as personal as a wedding, a christening, or a graduation. Its style will be decided by the requirements of the church, the wishes of the family, and the accepted ways of grieving in the family and community.

Despite these differences, there are some basic elements found in nearly every funeral service:

—The viewing of the body at the visitation or wake, or just prior to the funeral service;

—A funeral service or memorial service, with a tribute to the one who has died and a review of his or her life;

—Cards, flowers, letters, and gifts of food as expressions of sympathy, help, and support for the bereaved;

—A committal service at the cemetery or mausoleum;

—A shared meal for family and friends who have participated in the funeral;

—A reminder, in the Christian funeral, of the message of resurrection and hope.

70

These specific parts of the ceremony make the funeral ritual important. Together they help the family and friends of the one who has died acknowledge the ending in their lives and begin the transition to a new stage of life.

The Visitation

The visitation or wake, with the body on view, often precedes the funeral service. This may be a formal visitation in a church, a funeral home, or the deceased's home; it may be a private time in the hospital room or home when the family can be alone with their dead. In seeing the body, perhaps touching it, and finding life absent, we experience an ending. This may be a time for saying final goodbys, asking forgiveness, or expressing love, fear, loneliness, or anger. This is a time to realize the actuality of death. From a general knowledge that "people die," we can move to the specific that "grandma died."

We are physical beings. We grasp facts physically as well as intellectually. What we know only with our minds is less real to us than what we know with our whole being. What we can see, hear, or touch is more real to us than what we know because someone told us about it. For these reasons I am a strong believer in allowing the family to see, touch, hold, and talk to the body of a dead loved one. I greatly admire some hospital nurses I know who, in support of this idea, will leave family members alone in a hospital room with someone who has just died. The nurses delay their practice of dealing with the death until after the family has had some time and privacy.

We have already met Peter Harris. He was a young man with a son John, who was eight, and a daughter Sarah, who was four, when his long fight with Hodgkin's disease ended. Although both children had been aware of their father's illness for many years and had been involved in his care, John's attitude toward his father changed during the last weeks of the illness. For almost a month John refused to visit his father in the hospital and avoided him during the periods when Peter was able to be at home. Peter died in the hospital, by choice.

I called Janet to see how she was. "Are you taking the children to the funeral and the visitation?" I asked.

"Oh, I don't think so," she said. "Sarah is too young to know the difference, and John has been avoiding his dad for the past several weeks."

"Why don't you ask the children if they want to go?" I suggested. "If they don't, I wouldn't push them, but I think you should give them a chance to go if they want to."

Janet took my advice. She called me about a week after the funeral. "You know, Ruth," she said, "I'm so glad you suggested I ask the kids if they wanted to go to the funeral! John jumped at the chance! He went right up to the casket, straightened Peter's collar, and looked at him for a while. He sat beside me and held my hand through the whole funeral service. Since then, he's been more relaxed and a lot calmer."

Seeing the body for himself was an important part of John's dealing with his father's death. The illness had been a major part of his life for a long time. Toward the end, the illness seemed to be more than John could bear. He avoided visiting his father and avoided seeing him get weaker and weaker. Now it was all over. His father was dead. He would no longer have to deal with the fact of the illness. Death had been anticipated and even looked for. Now that it was here, John could face it. He could say "Goodby" to his father—and with that goodby also bid farewell to the way of life that surrounded his father's illness. John was ready for a new beginning.

Later in my telephone conversation with Janet Harris, she told me something else about John. "John has been going through the house, looking at his father's things. Just yesterday I found a box of Peter's things—pictures, medals, a pen—on John's dresser. He told me that these were the things of his dad's that he wanted to keep to remember him by."

After John had said goodby to his father, he moved easily and naturally to the step of putting together for himself a memory with which he could live. He looked through family photograph albums; he rummaged through drawers and boxes, looking at the things his father had saved; from among these he chose the ones he wanted to keep. He put them into a box and took them to his room.

The Purpose of Memory

When someone we love dies, it leaves a big hole in our world.

There is an emptiness inside which even seems to be reflected in the world around us. We cannot live with this gaping hole, anymore than we can survive with a torn artery pumping out our life blood. The artery must be tied or sutured; the void inside must be filled.

One way of filling the void left by a death is to build up a memory of the loved one that can become a part of our lives. In story and legend, one who is dying sees his whole life flash before him; the same sort of thing happens when we lose someone we love. Consciously and unconsciously, we review his life and piece together a memory that becomes a part of us.

There are many ways to do this, as John Harris demonstrated. We may look at family photograph albums, reread letters, handle personal treasures. We may listen to the loved one's favorite records, read his favorite books, sing his favorite songs. We may spend time with other friends who knew him and share memories with them. In this way we can make the transition from "before grandma died" to "after grandma died." Although grandma is no longer an active part of our daily living, we have a memory of her that in some way replaces her and becomes a part of us and of life without her. In this way the wound begins to heal, the emptiness to disappear.

Death may be met with refusal and denial, however. Instead of replacing a living grandma with a memory of her the way she used to be, we may hold to a hope that she will return. Rather than gather and build memories, we may create dreams and fantasies of the way things will be "when grandma comes back." Perhaps these dreams and hopes are somewhat inevitable. They can serve a temporary need to deny grandma's death and help us to hold off dealing with this death until we are more ready. However, there should be a progression from "when grandma comes back," to "if grandma comes back," to "if she could only come back!" and the realization that she will not return.

The final nature of death is difficult to grasp. Even when we feel we "know" it, our hand will reach out for the telephone to call grandma, we will remember a joke to share with her, or we will sit down and start to write her a letter. The fact of death becomes real gradually, through many situations in which we experience again the absence of the one who died.

This process holds especially true for children up to age ten or eleven. It is easy for a child to fantasize that "daddy has gone on a trip" or "grandpa is living at the hospital." Sometimes the adults in a child's life reinforce these fantasies. Thinking to ease the child's pain and grief, they only postpone his realization of the finality of death, interfere with his process of testing the meaning of that death, and thus delay the process of healing. Until the child begins to understand that daddy is dead and won't come back, he cannot begin to do the work of mourning. His understanding of daddy's death will be helped as he realizes again and again that "daddy isn't there" and is gently reminded, "No, he's not here. He died."

FROM "BEFORE" TO "AFTER"

The child who continues to deny the death of a loved one remains suspended in the transition period. He cannot go back to the old way of life, for it no longer exists; but he cannot go forward, either. He lives in a fantasy world, waiting endlessly for "everything to be all right" and unable to take the steps that would bring him healing.

Seeing the body is helpful to the child in accepting death. It can also serve as a reference point during the time he is testing and absorbing the reality of his loss. A child can discern the difference between a lifeless form and a living person. It is one thing for a child to be told, "Grandma died"; it is quite another to see her still, silent body with his own eyes and to realize that she is unable to see him, hear him, answer him, or smile at him. Afterward, when the child asks, "Is grandma coming to my birthday party?" the answer can be, "No, grandma died. Remember? You saw her and went to her funeral."

Although a child's grief and mourning process will differ from an adult's, it is no less real and no less necessary. The death of a close friend or family member disrupts the child's life as well as the adult's; life does not continue as usual for the one anymore than for the other. The child, too, must make the transition from "before grandma died" to "after grandma died" in his own life. After the transition is made, the death of a loved one will become an important time marker for the child, as well as for the rest of the family. Attempts to shield a child from the reality of death, no matter how well-meaning in intent, only result in disrupting the process of grief and mourning that are necessary to healing.

The funeral proceedings can also help in the transition from "before" to "after." Besides emphasizing the ending, it can be a point of beginning to put together a memory to live with. Most funeral services include a eulogy or memorial of the life of the one who died. This can be a summary of the person's life and its meaning in the lives of his family, friends, and community. In most cases it is a celebration of his life. As people get together during the visitation, the wake, the funeral, and the funeral meal, they share their memories of the one who died. The music used during the funeral will be music this one has liked; favorite poems or Bible verses may be read; remarks from family, friends, and co-workers may serve to fill in the picture of his life.

A Fuller Picture

None of us knows even one other person completely. Each of our friends and loved ones has a portion of life that does not include us. During the funeral proceedings we are given an opportunity to see our loved one more completely. We gain a brief glimpse of him through the eyes of others who knew him in different ways. We may respond to the sharing of memories both by saying, "Yes! That's just like him! That's the kind of person he was!" and by thinking, "I never knew that about him. That's a part of him I never saw." This review of his life, this filling in of our picture of him, affirms his reality and the meaning of his life. Sometimes, in the shared remembering, the person who died may be more real and more alive for us than he has ever been before. We have a chance to look at this person, no longer taking for granted any part of what he was, with eyes that really see anew. As John Hillis's funeral did for me, this time can provide a fresh realization of how truly special and unique this person was and how privileged we were to have known him.

Children may be particularly limited in their knowledge of the one who died. They may have known him only as "daddy," "uncle," or "John." For them especially, the sharing of memories and anecdotes from other family members, friends, co-workers, and neighbors can serve to enlarge the picture. As they see the respect and affection of his family, the special things other friends appreciated in him, the way he was thought of at work, they can experience a pride in knowing him and being related to him. They may see grandpa as a father, a neighbor, a salesman, and outdoorsman; they may realize that "mommy" was also a daughter, a sister, a friend. This can form the basis of a memory of grandpa or mommy that will be able to grow with them as they grow and become a part of their future as well as their past. Although they will outgrow the four-year-old or ten-year-old child's relationship to the one who died, they will have the basis for a memory and a knowledge of this person that they will then be able to relate to as an adolescent and later as an adult.

Melissa Barnes was another child who acted out in a visible way the work of putting together a memory of a dead loved one. Melissa, the oldest child of Steve and Pamela Barnes, was eleven when her father died.

Steve Barnes had surgery for colon cancer the summer that Melissa was nine. For almost a year Steve was well; then the cancer reappeared. Surgery, chemotherapy, and radiation were all tried, without success. Melissa and her brothers and sister all knew that daddy had cancer and they also learned that he would probably never get better. During his last year of life, although he had some periods of good health, Steve was steadily growing weaker and losing weight. He lived at home throughout his illness and continued to work and travel until the last three or four weeks. Both Steve and Pamela believed he should stay at home as long as possible, and they were both comfortable with the idea that he might die at home.

I had asked the Barnes if I could make a home visit to discuss future treatment, hospitalization, and other matters. It seemed to me that he was very close to death. We had an appointment for 9:30 on a Thursday morning. I dropped Jimmy off at nursery school and drove to the Barnes's.

As I was getting out of my car, Pamela ran from the house to meet me. "Please come upstairs right away, Ruth! I don't know what's happening, but Steve is breathing funny and he won't answer me!" We ran upstairs together. I found Steve lying in bed, yellow with jaundice and unconscious. He was breathing very irregularly and several times stopped temporarily. Pam threw herself across him on the bed and talked to him, begging him to wake up. I sat in a chair beside the bed and held his hand. In less than twenty minutes, Steve stopped breathing entirely. I sat still for a short while longer, then told Pam, "He's gone."

I went down to the kitchen, leaving Pam alone with Steve. She joined me in a few minutes. As she put on a pot of coffee, she called her father, asking him to come and to bring the older children from school. We drank coffee and talked, waiting for them to arrive. When the children got home, Pam took them upstairs, one at a time, to see their dad. Besides Melissa there were Jason, nine, and Jennifer, seven. Frederick, age four, was still at nursery school.

When I said that I would go get Frederick, Melissa volunteered to come along.

"I'm sorry, Melissa," I said in the car. "I really liked your dad."

She gave me half a smile and nodded. The rest of the way we were quiet. When we got to the nursery school, Melissa ran inside to get Frederick. She put her arms around him and said, "Daddy just died."

On the ride home we talked a little. Melissa asked why her father had died and why he hadn't gone to the hospital. I explained that he would not have gotten better at the hospital and gave her a brief explanation of the cause of his death.

Back at the house, Frederick and his mother went up to the bedroom, and the rest of the children visited with their grandparents and me in the kitchen and family room.

All the children were at the funeral. They spent part of the time visiting with cousins they hadn't seen for several months, and part of the time with the adults, watching and listening.

After the funeral I kept in touch with Pam for several months, talking with her on the phone and going over to the house for coffee. On one visit I arrived just as the children were coming home from school. Melissa approached me and asked, "Would you like to see some pictures of my dad?" I agreed, and Melissa took me on a tour of the house. She showed me all the pictures of Steve that she could find, commenting on each one: "He was fat then." "That one was in Hawaii." "Do you like this picture? I don't!" "This one is my favorite."

Melissa was doing the same kind of thing John Harris had done. She had gone around looking at the pictures of her father and was using them to help her form her own picture of him to remember him. Shortly after the funeral I wrote a letter to the Barnes children, telling them what I had known of their father and what kind of man I had found him to be. Besides adding to their memory, it helped me to put together a memory of their father for myself.

Time Alone

In reflecting on these funerals, another important fact has become obvious to me. Children need time alone as well as time for sharing. The hospital nurses whom I respect and admire acknowledge this when they discreetly leave a grieving family alone in the room with a loved one who has just died. Pamela Barnes spent time alone with Steve just after he died; she took her children up to him one at a time, so they too could be alone. At his father's visitation, John Harris went directly to the casket, alone, and was by himself with his father's body.

Goodbys between people who love each other have a very private and personal side. Whenever my husband or I leaves home, each of the children must come to say goodby with hugs and kisses. A general goodby to both of them, as I walk out to the garage, brings them both running, accusing me of not telling them goodby properly! So too with death. I believe it is instinctive to want to be alone with our dead, if only for a short while, in order to say our private goodby.

Each relationship is different. Every person brings a slightly different self to each of his relationships. Although all those who care about a person experience a loss at his death, this loss is different for each one. Part, perhaps even most, of the grief of the loss can be shared; part of it is private and individual. So there must be room in the funeral proceedings for each one who shares in the loss to have some privacy, some time alone. This may be no more than time at the casket or a solitary walk around the funeral home, looking at the flowers and reading the cards. Periods of silence during the funeral service can also give each person present a time to be alone with thoughts and memories.

Sharing Grief and Comfort

At least part of each person's grief can be shared, however. The sharing of grief and the resultant sharing of comfort are other functions of the funeral. This is an occasion for the family and friends to draw together. Even people who are normally nondemonstrative will usually take this time to hug each other, put an arm around one another, or hold each other's hands. Tears are shared, and smiles and laughter as well. In sharing affection for the one who died, in caring for his memory, in remembering him, people are drawn to one another. Our caring makes us belong to the community of those who knew and loved the one who died.

At John Hillis's funeral, our family experienced a closeness with friends of John's we had never met before. We belonged, because we cared about John and wanted to remember him. While John was alive, we had cared about him; now that John was dead, we still cared about his memory.

When we speak of the "communion of saints" in the Apostles' Creed, we refer to more than just an earthly, temporal community. We belong to a larger company, made up of those living and dead who share our faith. Those who have died live on in this community, and they live on in our memories. The celebration of the Eucharist as part of the Anglican funeral service emphasizes this aspect of community. There is the comfort of the shared meal and the belief that we participate, not only with those we can see around us, but also with those who have been part of this community on earth in the past.

Pat's story illustrates the importance of belonging to the community of those who cared about the one who died. When Pat was eight, her grandmother died. She had been close to her grandmother, although they lived in different towns. She enjoyed visiting grandma, and looked forward to her letters and phone calls. Pat's parents didn't tell her that her grandmother had died; when they left town to attend grandma's funeral, Pat stayed home. About two weeks later, Pat accidentally discovered that her grandmother had died.

Just a few months after her grandmother's death, Pat experienced a second loss. A favorite aunt was in the hospital. Pat knew the aunt was very ill, but was never told she was dying. One Sunday afternoon, Pat, dressed in her First Communion white, was sneaked up the back stairs of the hospital to her aunt's room. "I never saw her again," Pat said. "When she died, they didn't tell me. I felt somehow that I had stopped belonging to the family."

When I met Pat, she was twenty-eight and dealing with the

impending death of her father. However, when she told me of her grandmother's death, it was the eight-year-old girl speaking. "Why did they leave me out? Why didn't they tell me? Even then, I wanted to scream at my mother, 'Why didn't you tell me grandma died? Why didn't you take me along?'"

Pat suffered grief when her grandmother and her aunt died. The grief was compounded by the distress and hurt of being left out. She was isolated in her grief, with no one to talk to and no one to turn to for comfort. Twenty years later, as she faced the death of her father, she had to finish the work of mourning for her aunt and grandmother that she had never been able to do as a child.

A Sense of Belonging

In the sharing of the funeral, visitation, wake, and burial services, this sense of belonging can be emphasized. Those who attend a funeral are those who "belong" to the family as relatives and friends. Because they care for the memory of the one who has died, they have a common ground. Other barriers between these individuals become unimportant, at least for this period of time, as they embrace, cry, hold each other's hands, and share their loss and grief. Each one who grieves the loss of this person is less alone because of the others who share in it. They are not isolated in their grief or alone with their memories as long as there are others around who knew and loved the one they have known and loved.

Children need the comfort and security of this belonging. When they are included in the funeral services, it emphasizes their place in the family or as friends of the family. It may help them feel that they are a part, not only of the family, but also of the large circle of friends.

Belonging means sharing both the good and the bad. In the musical *Oliver* there is a delightful song, "Consider Yourself."

> Consider yourself one of us!
> If it should chance to be
>   that we should see
>   some harder days,
>   empty larder days,
>   why grouse?
> If we should chance to find
>   somebody to foot the bill,
>   why the drinks are on the house!

Being part of the family means that we get yelled at sometimes. Being part of the family means that we share the pain and discomfort of uncertain times.

I am reminded of a catchword in a family I came to be a part of. Since "dad" would often invite people over to dinner at the last minute, "mom" didn't always know ahead of time how many people would be sharing the meal. Although she could do miracles in stretching food, sometimes the size of the party exceeded even her ability to stretch. So the "secret signal": At times like this, "mom" would whisper to us, "F. H. B." F. H. B. meant "Family hold back." If there wasn't enough food, the company would be fed; the family ate lightly. You had to belong to be in on the secret, and to share going without, in order for there to be enough food.

Even a very young child—two or three years old—can sense when he is being treated carefully, like "company" rather than family. With the children I have known, I consider the relationship between us secure when we are free to yell at each other. As long as the children treat me with company manners, I know I'm not completely accepted; this works in reverse as well. By the same token, children who belong to the family have as much right to share with the family in grief and sorrow as they do in happiness and success.

THE CHRISTIAN AFFIRMATION

Unique to a Christian funeral is the affirmation of the Resurrection and the hope of eternal life. This is eloquently illustrated in the Episcopal Church, in which the Easter service is used for a funeral. A Christian funeral emphasizes the transition in the life of the one who has died: His life on earth is ended, his work on earth is finished, and he has gone on to a new life. For him the transition is the move from Good Friday to Easter Sunday.

A Christian funeral holds out the hope of meeting again. For those who are left behind, there is the knowledge that they too will make the journey from this life to the next. This is different from denying the fact of death, from waiting for the loved one to come back. Rather, it is the statement that, though he cannot come back to us, we have the hope of going to him.

Grasping Spiritual Truths

Although children often seem to have difficulty grasping abstract truths, this does not, in my experience, hold true when it comes to spiritual realities. I have been amazed to see the way in which young children seem to grab hold of these truths, often more easily and completely than their elders.

In our home, mealtime discussions often become theological or philosophical. We have tried to take every opportunity to teach our children the meaning of the Christian faith and to weave it into the fabric of everyday life. Because death is a familiar subject in our house, given our vocations, we had already talked about dying, heaven, and Jesus' coming again before Juanita was four. Juanita had expressed a decided preference for having Jesus come back while she was still alive, so she wouldn't have to die!

Shortly after Juanita's fourth birthday, we attended the funeral of the man who had been my husband's pastor while Jim was in college. Juanita attended the funeral with us. She sat quietly through the church service and the ride to the cemetery. At the graveside, Juanita looked at the grave, the casket, and the people gathered around. Then she looked at her father and said, "Daddy, if Jesus came again right now, they wouldn't have to finish burying Dr. Harvey, would they?"

Even a three-or-four-year-old can be told about heaven and the Resurrection in a form he can begin to understand. Questions that arise about death, funerals, burial, and cremation should be answered simply, by an adult whom the child loves and trusts. It is always better to say "I don't know" than to make up information to answer a child's questions, however. We can share with children only the knowledge and faith that we ourselves possess.

FIRST EXPERIENCES

It is obvious that I believe children can and should be included in funerals. Most children are ready to participate in funeral services as soon as they begin to take part in other church services. By the age of five, I believe—although some authorities would say age seven—most children can sit through a funeral service and learn from it.

Children will not be upset by funeral proceedings if they are with an adult they know and trust and if they are allowed to learn at their own pace. If a child is allowed to sit and watch when he doesn't feel ready to participate, and if he is not held back from participation when he feels ready, the funeral itself will not be upsetting.

"Sights and Sounds"

Part of a child's education regarding death is the introduction to the "sights and sounds" of a funeral. Since many funerals and visitations take place in a mortuary, or funeral home, the child should be allowed to visit one. Anything that gives a child an opportunity to learn about the places and customs surrounding funerals can help eliminate fear and uncertainty due to strangeness when the real time comes.

I recommend taking a child to the funeral of a church member in his own church as a first experience. This can be done at age three or four, or as soon as the child's age and behavior do not produce an undue strain on the parent. Before and after the service, the child can be given an opportunity to make comments and ask questions about what transpires and about the surroundings.

The next step may be to take the child to a funeral or a visitation at a mortuary. This should be a funeral or visitation the adult would have attended anyway, but one in which the child does not have a close emotional involvement. This can give the child an opportunity to visit the mortuary and to look at the body if he wants to. A child should not be forced to look at the body; however, if the opportunity is offered, the natural curiosity of young children is such that they will usually do so.

The first funerals that my children attended were funerals of people they had known only slightly, if at all. They came as part of the family, starting about age four, because my husband or I wanted to go. The children had been in several different funeral homes; they had visited cemeteries and a mausoleum; they had been to funeral services in different settings. By the time they attended the funeral of John Hillis, whom they knew and loved, they were already familiar with the physical environment. They did not have to deal with strange proceedings in a strange surrounding at the same time that they were experiencing personal grief.

When Mr. Allen died, I went to his visitation. He had been my patient during the final weeks of his illness, and I wanted to share the funeral with the family. I gave Jimmy, then five, the choice of coming with me or staying home with a babysitter, and he chose to come along. He was very interested in the visitation; he made several trips up to the casket to see and feel the body. (I later found him talking to the mortician, asking if he could see the vein they had used to inject the embalming fluid!) The visitation didn't upset or frighten Jimmy; he looked at and handled the body by his own choice. This was not a quiet, dignified visitation, either; some members of the Allen family were loud and hysterical in expressing their grief.

Once a child has experienced a funeral without the emotional involvement attached to the death of a personal friend or a loved one, he can be included in funerals the family plans or attend those he expresses a desire to attend. These can be left to the child's choice. If he prefers not to go, he should probably be allowed to stay home. In these matters I follow the same guidelines for taking children to weddings, graduations, and other ceremonies.

Our children have accompanied my husband and me on hospital rounds and house calls. Therefore they have come to know some of our patients fairly well. When one of these patients dies, we ask the children if they would like to attend the funeral.

Mrs. O'Brien was the director of the children's choir at church. Juanita was in the choir for two years before Mrs. O'Brien had to resign due to illness. Six months later, she died. Juanita, then seven, was insistent that she be taken to the funeral. "She was my teacher, and I loved her. I want to go to her funeral." Attending the funeral gave Juanita a chance to show her love for Mrs. O'Brien; she was comforted by being allowed to take part in the service.

I really came to understand how important it can be for a child to attend a funeral a year later, however, when we missed one. Mr. Martin was practically a fixture at the children's school. Since his retirement, he had devoted much of his time to handyman work at the school. He was there frequently and came to know many of the children. When he became ill, the children made cards for him. Juanita made a special valentine box of cookies and candies for him, "to say 'Thank you' for all the things he does for us."

When Mr. Martin died, the schoolchildren were given time off to attend the funeral. Juanita asked if I would take her. I agreed, but through a series of delays, I was late; we arrived at the church just after the funeral procession had left for the cemetery. I apologized to Juanita for missing the funeral. "That's all right, mommy," she answered. However, she was very quiet on the way home. When she was back home, she flew up to her room and flung herself across her bed, sobbing. Something was missing. She had not been able to finish dealing with Mr. Martin's death.

About thirty minutes later, Juanita called me to come up to her room. She pointed to the wall beside her bed. There she had posted a sign on red construction paper with a bright green border. It read, "In memory of my dearly beloved friend, Mr. Martin, who died January 23, 1981." Her eyes and cheeks were still wet with tears, yet she was smiling. "Now I have something to remember him by," she explained.

I was fortunate in that Juanita had already developed resources of her own in dealing with loss and grief. Although I robbed her of the opportunity to use the funeral to come to terms with Mr. Martin's death, she used her own imagination and instincts to find another way. She said her own goodby to him and found a way to keep a memory of him. I believe I made a mistake in allowing us to miss the funeral; however, it was not a fatal mistake—not because of anything I did to remedy it, but because of the coping abilities that Juanita had already developed before this happened.

5 // HELPING A CHILD TO GRIEVE

A CHILD'S ABILITY TO COPE with loss and the grief it brings depends first of all on the adult who is trying to help. This adult may be a parent, a close friend, a grandparent, an aunt or uncle, or a teacher. To help a child, the adult must have a relationship with him based on his love and trust of the adult and the adult's acceptance of him. The more completely the adult accepts the child—the more the child feels that he is valued and loved for himself—the greater the influence the adult can have. Accepting the child means accepting his immaturities, faults, abilities, feelings, and strengths —that is, all that the child is, just the way he is. It translates into the statement, "I love you just the way you are, because you are you," without conveying the sense of any hidden "but" tacked on.

Besides this relationship between the child and the adult, several other factors influence the degree to which an adult will be a help and positive guide. An adult is most effective if he has learned to cope with grief in his own life. The attitudes and actions of the adult will be a strong influence. An adult who has faced personal grief, who has come to terms with personal loss and has grown through it, who has come to terms with death—even the fact of his own eventual death—is the one who is most able to help a child in these situations.

A HELPING RELATIONSHIP

A number of feelings and attitudes are common to the various adults involved with children who are experiencing grief. The adult will find it necessary to deal with his own denial of the child's loss; his own grief over the hurt the child is feeling; his own feelings of

87

grief if he shares in the child's loss; and his own feelings of helplessness, frustration and anger, guilt and relief. The way he is able to deal with his own feelings will influence his ability to help the child.

Feelings of grief are uncomfortable and distressing to both children and adults. A child's reaction to these "bad" feelings is often that he feels bad about himself. He turns to the adults he loves and trusts to tell him whether or not these "bad" feelings mean that he is "bad." By accepting the child, the adult communicates the information that it is all right to have "bad" feelings and that having them does not make a person "bad."

The "Child" in Us

However, the adult's reactions to the child's grief and feelings of "badness" is complicated by the fact that these feelings also exist in the adult. No matter how "grown-up" we are, there is still a little child in each of us. This "child" in us responds with grief to the child's grief. Furthermore, the adult's "child" is burdened with the memories of other griefs and other losses, brought sharply into focus by the child's pain.

When the "child" within the adult experiences afresh his own remembered grief, it may trigger a "parent" response to the grief—one learned by the adult when he himself was a child. As adults we may "become" the adults who responded to our childhood grief and react as they did:

—We may turn to the child in anger and accusation, blaming him for his part in the loss: "Why can't you be more careful? Can't you ever remember your homework? This is the third time this week you've forgotten it at Bobby's house!"

—We may give the child a short sermon, helping him to "learn a lesson" from his loss: "No, I'm not going back to the playground to look for your baseball cap. You know you shouldn't just lay your clothes on the ground when you're playing! Now you'll just have to live without it. Next time maybe you'll remember to take better care of your belongings!"

—We may shrug off the child's loss, dismissing his reactions of grief as unimportant: "You mean you want me to drive all the way back for that picture? It's just a picture! You can draw another one anytime! If you really wanted it, you should have put it in your backpack, and you'd have it now! Don't carry on like that about a little thing like a picture, or I may give you something real to cry about!"

Any of these responses (a little exaggerated in these examples) tends to reinforce the child's feelings that there is something wrong with him, that the pain of his grief really means that he is "bad" or "no good."

None of these responses is completely uncalled-for or necessarily all wrong. If the instructions can be given in the form of suggestions rather than a sermon and can come after the child's grief has been accepted as legitimate and real by the adult, they may be of value to the child. It is part of an adult's role to help a child learn to discriminate, to achieve perspective, to differentiate between major and minor losses. This function can be served without altogether dismissing the child's feelings of grief. If the grief really is disproportionate to the loss, this can be discussed with the child after an initial period of accepting his grief and offering him comfort.

Dealing With "Little Deaths"

I cannot stress too strongly that it is important for any adult wishing to help a child to take the child's own evaluation of the losses seriously. This means learning to recognize the "little deaths" in the child's life (see chapter 2) and accepting them as real losses, producing real grief. The adult may or may not feel any grief himself over these losses, and he may relive a similar loss situation from the past. As the adult takes the child's loss and grief seriously, the child's affection, time, and caring are accepted as valid. It is fitting to mourn the loss of a water-color picture that has taken the child half an hour to produce, which was intended as a surprise for daddy or grandma, but which the wind snatched from the child's hand and blew away.

An insidious method of discounting a child's loss is the response, "Be a big girl! Don't cry!" or "Be a brave little man and dry those tears!" or "You're too big to cry!" It is more common for us to forbid tears to boys than to girls, but there is a prevalent attitude in our society that tears are for the weak, the timid, the "babies." Since tears are the natural physiological outlet for many types of emotions, we begin to deprive our children almost from the moment of birth to give up a very normal physical way of bringing release and healing if we teach them not to cry.

When we can conquer the tendency to dismiss the child's loss as insignificant and learn to give him permission to cry (and this is harder than it sounds!), we are faced with the need to comfort him. Again, there are some nearly automatic responses: "Don't cry, honey, mommy will kiss the knee and it will be all better" or "Don't worry about losing the ballgame. It was just a game anyway. Look, I made your favorite dinner—pork chops, mashed potatoes, and lima beans, and guess what? There's a lemon pie for dessert!" We may say, "It was just a plastic headband. I'm sure they have them in all the department stores. We'll go out right after dinner and buy a new one" or "Don't cry about the ice cream cone. There's plenty of ice cream back in the store. We'll just go back and get you another one."

THE URGE TO ERASE SORROW

There is a strong desire within us to erase the child's sorrow, so we want to see his tears stop. We are also tempted to avert the child's pain—and our own discomfort—by distracting the child with food, toys, or special activities, or by rushing out for a replacement.

Our role in helping a child cope with grief is not, however, that of a magic sponge, wiping away all traces of it. Rather, we are comforters. If we can "kiss the hurt," hold the child, or listen to him pour out his tears, pain, and anger, we can fill the role well. We kiss, hug, and listen to allow the child to express his feelings in an atmosphere of acceptance and caring, not to stop the pain. We allow him to work through the pain of healing. After all, the idea of comfort presupposes that some sorrow or hurt exists that needs to be healed.

It is especially important to avoid giving the child the impression that our listening, caresses, and love are based on the condition that he stop crying, feeling sad, and being angry. "Don't cry, let me kiss it all better" may be heard by the child as our way of saying, "If you stop crying, if you stop feeling sad, I will love you. If you keep on crying or feeling sad, I will stop loving you." If we truly accept the child, we will give him neither the message "You can't cry" nor the message "You must cry." We will allow him the freedom to find a way of expressing grief that satisfies his needs.

As adults we tend to feel helpless and vulnerable when a child is grieving. We tend to be more fiercely protective of our children, their rights, their possessions, and their feelings than we are even of our own. We may feel, "That's not fair! He's so little! He shouldn't have to go through this!" (even if, at the same time, we tend to blame the child for the loss!). We would like to turn back the clock and relive the situation so as to prevent the child's loss and distress. I vividly remember feeling this way when Juanita missed her event in the tricounty swim meet. How I wished I could go back fifteen or twenty minutes! I would be sure Juanita was there, in the bullpen, ready for her event; she would get to swim and compete for the medal.

Guilt and Responsibility

Just as feelings of guilt almost inevitably arise amid feelings of grief in a child, so they do in adults. Our "child" feels the two simultaneously or in quick succession. If something has gone wrong, if someone is unhappy, then someone is to blame. Even as we blame the child, we also tend to blame ourselves. We feel (and are, to a certain degree) responsible for our children—for their health, their comfort, their safety, their happiness. If something "bad" has happened to them, we must be at fault in some way. As parents we tend to believe that a child's illness, failures in school or sports, pain, anger, and sorrow could have been prevented. It is our job to take care of them; this means, to our minds, we are supposed to keep them healthy, smart, popular, and happy. We tend to ignore the fact that the child has some responsibility for his own achievements and happiness; we look on happiness as a child's right, not a choice. To a greater or lesser degree, we measure our own success and adequacy as parents by the contentment of our children.

Emotional turmoil and upheavals, in our lives and in our children's, are often the labor pains preceding the birth of new understanding, compassion, and maturity. They may be the means of eliminating bad and harmful elements from our lives; they may serve to cut out something good to make room for something even better. If we have "skins" that conceal the real person inside, the events in life that bring the shedding of these skins are necessary, however painful they are. If this is true for adults, it holds true for our children also.

God's Model for Parenting

When we feel like "bad" parents because of our children's distress, it is time to consider our ideal of parenthood. There is only one completely adequate, reliable model of parenting, and that is God. He is Father/Mother, the ultimate Parent. As we become familiar with God's dealings with His children, in the stories of the Bible and in the lives of people around us, we can see that He allows (some say "causes") His children to experience pain and suffering and to wrestle with difficulties. He is present as a Comforter and Guide, but His intervention in difficult times more often takes the form of helping us learn to deal with the troubles and trials than of removing them.

This is the parenting model offered to us by God. It should be a help and a comfort to us when we choose to let our children deal with their problems, great or small—the stubborn shoelaces that continually escape from four-year-old fingers, or the death of a beloved pet. We are to be present to comfort and guide as needed, but not take over the situation from the child with a view toward avoiding or removing the problem.

An adult intending to help a child learn to cope with grief must accept his own feelings as well as the child's. This involves the willingness to endure our own discomfort along with the child's and to put up with the disruption of life wrought by the child's expressions of grief. Enduring a child's pain requires also that we be willing to endure the pain of our own helplessness, frustration, and anger. It includes facing realistically our feelings of guilt and sometimes the need to tend to real guilt.

Helping a child learn to deal with loss and grief is rewarding. It can result in a stronger, more mature, more compassionate, and more resourceful child. However, it is often a turbulent process. It is much easier and more peaceful to flush the dead goldfish down the toilet and replace it with a lively new fish while the child is napping than to go through the tears, anger, and questions the child will have when he sees his goldfish floating dead in the fish bowl.

POSITIVE PATTERNS OF GRIEVING

In dealing with a child's grief, it is almost always better to act first, then listen, and then talk. Our intuitive responses are more likely to be helpful than the responses we reason and think out. The replays from our "parent"—the responses we learned from adults when we were children—are also more likely to take the form of words. A typical reaction to a grieving child is to meet him with open arms, hug him tightly, pick him up, and hold him. This is a physical, tangible way of telling the child, "I'm here. I love you. I know you are hurting." The adult's instinct to shield the child with his arms and body is mirrored in the child's instinct to run to a parent's arms when hurt or in trouble. The total-body embrace of the child is a vivid picture of the total acceptance he is seeking in his hurt and the total acceptance we want to offer him.

At age nine or ten, a child may begin to be embarrassed by this urge to run into mom or dad's arms for comfort and security. He may feel he is getting "too old" for that "kid stuff." Mom and dad may also feel some hesitation and embarrassment, because they too wonder whether the child is uncomfortable with such a physical show of affection. Although we are *never* too old to need hugs and kisses and other physical expressions of love, many children do go through a stage when physical displays of affection make them feel uncertain and uncomfortable. For such a child, a brief hug, an arm around the shoulder, or a pat on the back may be all the physical response the adult should offer. When the child begins to withdraw from the embrace, it is probably best to let him go.

Wanting to Talk

Another instinctive response to a grieving child is to hold him on the lap and wait for him to tell us what happened. For extremely verbal adults, the hardest part is waiting for the child to talk—if he wants to—without prying or putting words in his mouth. Our physical posture can tell the child a lot about our acceptance of him and our willingness to let him grieve in his own way. If we can hold him gently on our lap, relaxed, perhaps rocking, without talking or asking questions, he will feel free to talk or be silent as he chooses. On the other hand, if we are stiff, impatient, and consciously waiting while we hold him, the child will feel that something is expected of him and will attempt to do or say the "right" thing.

An older child who is uncomfortable being held will nevertheless read our "body language." We may sit in a chair, on the floor, or on the kitchen counter, relaxed and at ease. Our body itself says to the child, "I'm here if you want me. Talk if you wish, or be silent; it's okay." To sit stiffly, stand at attention, pace nervously, or fidget says to the child, "I'm busy and in a hurry. I don't have all night. Hurry up and get this over with!" Again, the child will sense that we expect something from him. He may try hard to meet our expectations, or he may become belligerent and withdrawn, feeling that we "wouldn't understand" or "don't care anyhow."

Talking about his grief is most effective if the conversation is initiated by the child and if he feels free to stop the discussion when he wishes. Sometimes we need to open the conversation, however, for the child to be sure that it is all right to talk. In this case, a question like "Is there something you feel like talking about?" can be effective. The child should be given the right to say, "No, I don't think so" or, "Maybe, but not right now." Many times the child needs our sympathetic presence more than he needs a listening ear—and much more than he needs explanations and advice.

It may become necessary for us to express in words that we accept his personal pattern of grieving and not rely solely on non-verbal expression.

Doubts About the Pattern

Sometimes we are completely accepting of the child's pattern of grieving, only to discover that the child himself cannot accept his personal way of expressing grief as "right" and "normal." Like my son Jimmy, this child may compare his own behavior and feelings with the grief behavior he has seen or inferred in others. If there are many discrepancies between what he feels and does and what he sees in others, he may feel that he is not grieving or that there is something "wrong" with his way of grieving.

The child of four or five or older may need explicit verbal permission from an adult he loves and trusts in order to feel that his way of expressing grief is "okay." We may need to tell the child, "It's all right to cry if you feel like it; crying is for big people as well as for children," or the child may need to hear the opposite, "If you don't feel like crying, that's all right. Sometimes the sadness we feel inside just can't come out in tears."

This holds true for the other feelings involved in grief: anger, relief, guilt. We may need to tell the child, "I think you might be feeling angry because you lost the race. It's all right to feel angry if we miss something important to us" or "I know you loved your dog. I expect you feel sad that he got hit by a car. Maybe you feel a little bit as if it were your fault; maybe you wonder if you could have taken better care of him, so he wouldn't have been hit and killed. When accidents like that happen, lots of people wonder if things could have been different, and if they could have prevented the accident" or "Even though we miss grandma and are sad she died, it is a relief to have our Saturdays free again. I wonder if you have been feeling glad that now we can have Saturday as a family day, instead of going to the nursing home to see grandma." This sort of verbal permission for the child to feel the way he does may be followed by a chance for the child to respond. If we are guessing at a child's feelings, he needs a chance to affirm or refute our guess. If it is a guess, we should make it clear to the child: "I think you might be angry because you lost the race" rather than "You must be very angry about losing the race."

If we express our own feelings and opinions, it leaves the child an opportunity to agree or disagree. When we tell him what he is feeling, he has a greater tendency to become hostile and defensive, ending the open communication between us, and making it more difficult for him to talk about his thoughts and feelings.

Another way to give a child permission to feel and express his feelings is by sharing our feelings with him. Short, simple statements without elaborate explanations are most effective. "You know, I feel bad about your dog's being hit by the car. I have wondered whether I was careful about closing the gate the last time I was in the back yard with him" or "I really miss grandma. I'm sorry she had to die. But you know, going to the nursing home every Saturday was really getting to me. I'm almost glad she died while I still had the strength and energy to keep on visiting her every week."

DISTRACTION AND REPLACEMENT

It is difficult for an adult to just stand back, refrain from interfering with a child's feelings or coping mechanisms, and allow him to experience his grief in his own way, according to his own timetable.

Two typical adult reactions by which we attempt to cope with our own discomfort in the face of a child's grief are distraction and replacement. Both of these can be helpful or harmful, depending mainly on timing. Immediate distraction may sidetrack the work of mourning, pushing it down to a subconscious or unconscious level. This can allow fantastic ideas and bizarre notions to flourish, un-examined in the light of reason and untested by the child's mind or the aid of adult understanding. A child's feelings about his own guilt or another's blame for the loss become accepted facts in the unconscious mind. Distraction offered later in the course of mourning, on the other hand, may serve to give the child a needed break from the difficult and painful task, renewing his resources, motivation, and courage to continue.

Immediate replacement may cause the child to deny the reality of a loss. He may accept the replacement as if it were in fact the thing he lost and thus fail to mourn the loss. Although this may not matter much in the case of an ice cream cone, a small toy, or a plastic headband, it can establish a pattern of dealing with loss that will become harmful as more serious losses are suffered. It also has the disadvantage, already discussed, of giving the child the impression that things and people are interchangeable, that nothing is unique or really special.

Yet, replacement and distraction do have a place in coping with a child's grief. Children tend to have a "short sadness span"—that is, their emotional and psychological make-up is such that they cannot sustain the feelings of grief or the work of mourning for a long, uninterrupted period of time. The work of mourning, even in adults, tends to be intermittent, broken by periods of near-normal life.

For a child, the breaks are usually longer and more frequent. The need for a break will vary with the child's age, his attention span, the severity of his grief, his physical condition, and his per-sonality. A child who is ill or fatigued will not be able to sustain feelings of grief and the work of mourning as long as he can when he is in good health and well rested. An intense, sensitive child will do his work of mourning in a very different manner from the relaxed, happy-go-lucky child.

A two-or-three-year-old may cry bitterly over a lost blanket, broken toy, or dead pet for five, ten, fifteen minutes, then turn around, all smiles, ready for the next item in his day. A five-or-six-year-old may be totally immersed in his grief and the work of mourning for as long as an hour, then appear to have forgotten his loss completely and continue "business as usual." The time at which the child spontaneously emerges from his sadness and work of mourning is the ideal time for distraction; this is the time to offer him an opportunity to try something new: drawing with pastels, playing a new recording, going for a walk, or reading a new book.

The Time for Replacement

Replacing the lost object should probably wait until the child is emotionally ready to risk new affection and new involvement. It may be that the child is ready for a replacement at the same time he is ready for distraction. After the loss of her headband, Juanita demanded that I stop immediately at the first possible place and buy her a new one. By the time we got home to Peoria, she had truly "given up" the headband she had lost. She had accepted and dealt with its loss. It was part of our trip to Dallas, and she had the memory of the headband, the way she had looked in it, and the pleasure it had given her. At that time she was ready for a replacement; she could go to the store and buy a new headband, no longer looking for the identical one she lost, but for something new that would in part replace it and remind her of our trip.

When we refuse to submit to a child's demands for immediate replacement of a lost object, we need to remember that we have an ally within the child himself. Even while the child is loudly demanding, "Stop at the next town and get me another pink headband!" there are feelings within that instinctively cry out, "But that's not the headband I lost!" The child's feelings about immediate replacement are ambivalent: He is trying to obliterate the memory and pain of loss with a replacement; but he also "knows" deep inside that nothing is truly identical, truly an adequate replacement. Replacement is best timed when it coincides with the child's realization that there is no true duplicate for what he lost, but he still wants something similar as a reminder.

TESTING THE LOSS

The rebound from grief and sadness and the abandonment of the work of mourning by a young child may fool us. We may decide that the child has completed his mourning because he is ready to turn to new activities; we may even feel baffled by the apparent shallowness of his feelings and the seeming indifference he displays toward what he lost. In fact, it may be that the feelings are so deep and the grief so painful that the child is unable to face it completely or to feel it for a long time. What we interpret as the end point of his grief and mourning process may merely be a stopping point along the way. He has not reached the end of his mourning; he has only stopped to rest a while.

The child is also probably involved in testing his loss, both its reality and its extent. His initial period of sadness and grief may accomplish the work of mourning for the facet of the loss that he has discovered, understood, and accepted. When this is completed, he will respond to distractions, become involved in new activities, or resume his familiar schedule.

But just as suddenly as the child has dried his tears and turned away from his grief, he may plunge right back into it, to our surprise and confusion. In the middle of the drawing he is making, or the record he is listening to, or the exhilaration of trying out dance steps to a lively new record, the child may seem suddenly to "remember" his grief. He again moves into his work of mourning, withdrawing from people, new activities, the normal routine, or the company of friends. This should not come as a surprise, although it often does. In fact, the child may have discovered a new facet of his loss and may then begin to grieve and mourn the same loss in a new light. Depending on the magnitude of the loss, the child may need several or many intervals of grief, interrupted by "breaks," as he does the work of mourning.

Mourning involves testing the reality of the loss; discovering its extent and the numerous intangible losses involved; "letting go" of the lost thing by accepting its absence for the present and future; compiling a memory of the lost thing; and recovering the emotional energy invested in what was lost. The work of mourning proceeds at the conscious and unconscious levels simultaneously, and many of the tasks listed occur simultaneously. The tasks of mourning may also tend to be cyclical, needing to be "repeated" when new intangible losses are uncovered or new effects of the loss are recognized.

The First Step of Mourning

Testing the reality of the loss is the first step in the work of mourning. When Jimmy lost his wallet, we spent several days looking in nooks and corners of the house, sorting through his accumulated "treasures," opening drawers and poking around in closets. At the end of each unsuccessful search, Jimmy and his family were more ready to believe that the wallet and money were gone.

When Juanita missed her event in the tri-county swim meet, the loss became real as she tried in various ways to be reinstated and failed. When the event was called, the gun went off, and the swimmers were in the water, her loss seemed final and real to her.

A large part of testing the reality of a loss for a child under nine involves his understanding of time, his concept of the future, and therefore his ability to accept the loss as permanent. The two-or-three-year-old may come to understand that a book is lost and may accept the loss the afternoon it happens. However, if it is a favorite book—perhaps the one he likes read to him at every bedtime—he may need to "learn" all over again that night that the book is lost. In this case it is not the reality of the loss the child is wrestling with, but the permanence of it. He does not lack understanding that the book is "gone"; he has an insufficient grasp of the meaning of the future to understand that the book is "all gone."

It may help an adult to be patient with the struggles of the two-to-five-year-old if he understands that the child is learning a lot about the meaning of the future and the concept of time. The child may understand and accept (with tears and grief) the fact that his Snoopy is lost at naptime; by bedtime, he may need to "learn" the loss of Snoopy all over again; this loss may need to be relearned once or twice or even at every naptime and bedtime for a number of days. This is not a case of refusing to deal with the loss, but rather one of beginning to connect the loss of Snoopy now and the absence of Snoopy later.

Physical Confirmations

Physical confirmations help a child greatly to accept a loss as real. This holds true for any child, but it is particularly important for the child under six. To help this child accept the fact that "blankey is all gone," it is more effective to "show" than merely to "tell." The adult may help the child look for his blanket—looking through the car, the house, the yard; calling grandparents and neighbors to find out if the child left it there; perhaps retracing the steps of an afternoon walk to be sure the "blankey" is really gone. The loss is more real and definite if the child can "see for himself" that the blanket is lost, than if mommy or daddy merely says it is.

A child under six may need to look for his lost "blankey" several times, even on different days, to realize that it is permanently gone. Even reminding the child of his search for the lost object yesterday may not be effective; if he has not yet learned the meaning of the future, he will not see any reason why the fact that the blanket was gone last time he looked for it should mean it is likely to be gone this time.

As the child searches in vain for what is lost, it can help him to have an adult along, one he loves and trusts. The adult's presence affirms the reality of the child's loss and also indicates to him that the adult takes the loss seriously. The child's feelings of grief are affirmed as acceptable and valid.

What to Tell a Child

What we tell a child also affects his testing of the reality of the loss and his ability to mourn it effectively. It is best to give a child truthful information, a little at a time, and repeat it as often as necessary.

It is easier for a child to understand and deal with the statement "Smokey died" or "Grandma died and was buried" than to have death explained in terms of a trip, sleep, or even "going to heaven." It is confusing for a child to be told, "Grandma went on a long, long trip" or "Grandpa fell asleep and didn't wake up." In the former case, the child will expect grandma to return, to send a postcard, or to call on the telephone. In the latter event, the child may become afraid of sleeping: "If grandpa fell asleep and never woke up, how do I know I will wake up tomorrow morning?" This child may resist naps; bedtime may become a fear-filled time of battle as he tries to avoid sleeping. Even children three or four years old already have an idea of death and seem to fear it. To connect a natural, expected event in the child's daily life with the idea of death, which he probably sees as some horrible monster, adds to his distress. Any explanation of death that leaves a question in the child's mind as to the reality of his loss will hinder him in his testing process and complicate his work of mourning.

The value of including the child in the visitation and funeral ceremonies of a loved one has already been discussed in chapter 5. If the loss involves a pet, the ritual of a funeral and burial for the pet in the back yard or in a flowerpot can help the child accept the reality of it. My children both held a brief funeral and burial for their pets when Jimmy's snake and Juanita's millipede died; the pets were buried in flowerpots inside the house. This made it easier for them to accept the reality of the deaths and to "let go" of the pets.

As Christians we may tell our children that "Uncle died and went to heaven" in an attempt to comfort them and make their grief easier to bear. However, if the child does not yet have a clear concept of heaven or the meaning of death, this may merely confuse him and delay his acceptance of reality. Even as Christian adults, we may be denying the reality of death and its losses in our misconceptions of heaven and eternal life. We may hide behind our faith as a substitute for dealing with the reality and (earthly) finality of death. A child may think of heaven as an earthly place and "going to heaven" the same as taking a trip to Chicago; telling him that grandma died and went to heaven has the same inherent difficulties as telling him that grandma went on a long trip.

Before we—adults and children—arrive at the comfort of knowing that grandma is in heaven, and believing that someday we can join her there, we must deal with her death as a permanent fact and a real loss. The fact that grandma is in heaven doesn't mean we don't miss her and don't feel sad; knowing that she is in heaven still doesn't make it possible for us to call her on the telephone, visit her, or get birthday cards from her. Our loss in terms of our life on earth is still permanent and final.

I believe we need an understanding of this dimension of death and loss before we can understand the hope of the Resurrection and the meaning of eternal life. The comfort comes to us in our need, our grief, our sorrow. If we deny the loss, we have no reason for grief and therefore for comfort. God is the God of comfort in our need, not in our denial of our loss.

Testing the reality of a loss for the older child is a matter of discovering its intangible losses and testing its permanence through yearly holidays and family activities. For the child six to nine and possibly older, the permanence of a loss may be realized in day-to-day activities, but even more sharply at holidays and special family times: Christmas, Thanksgiving, Easter, Independence Day, birthdays, family picnics, and vacations. The sudden recurrence of grief and the need for mourning on these occasions is not unusual and may even be expected.

THE PROBLEM OF WITHDRAWAL

During the period of mourning, the child may react to the discovery of new facets of his loss by withdrawing. This withdrawal provides protection for the child's feelings and allows him to use his emotional energy for mourning rather than for normal activities, interactions with friends and family, or planning for the future. The work of mourning is personal and private, and a child's withdrawal is a way of achieving the privacy he needs.

Depression is a form of withdrawal and of conserving emotional and physical energy. The child who seems depressed moves, talks, and thinks slowly, sleeps more than usual, and seems fatigued much of the time. He may lack the energy to move, talk, eat, or listen. There is nothing particularly harmful or abnormal about this type of reaction to grief. During this time, the child's work of mourning will continue, probably at a largely unconscious level. It is wise not to intrude on the withdrawn child; allow him his solitude and privacy.

However, the feelings of loneliness and isolation that often accompany grief can be painful. Without denying him his right to withdraw, an adult can still comfort the child by his presence and do much to relieve the feelings of loneliness. At the same time the child needs privacy and solitude, he also needs to know that he belongs, is accepted, and is loved. An adult may invite the child to come and sit in the kitchen or living room while the adult goes about his work. He may ask the child, "Would you like to come down to the kitchen and read there while I get supper?" If the child retreats to his room, the adult may knock on the door and ask, "Is it all right if I bring my magazine in here and read it?" or "Would you like to come into my room and read? I have some things I want to read too." Talking is more likely to be sensed by the child as an intrusion on his privacy than the physical presence of an adult he loves and trusts. We can help him maintain his privacy by respecting his silence, yet let him know by staying with him that he is not alone.

Bedtime may be especially difficult for the grieving child. At night our defenses are down; we are fatigued; problems, fears, and anxieties tend to loom larger than they do in the light of day. A parent may make it a habit to "tuck the child in" at night and hold his hand, rub his back, or just sit quietly close to him for a while.

By Themselves—But Not Alone

Some children indicate clearly that they want to be left to themselves but do not wish to be physically alone. After dinner, a child may pick up a book and sit in the kitchen, living room, or family room with the rest of the family, but keep himself apart by not joining into the activities of others. The child may be invited to join in, but he should not be nagged, pressured, or forced to do so. He should be accepted on his own terms.

With his "short sadness span," the withdrawal of a child is not likely to be prolonged. He may spontaneously set down the book he is holding and say, "Deal me in on the next game of Uno." He may begin to join in the family conversation, share an amusing incident from school, or relate a new joke. At this time the child is ready for a break from his work of mourning or may have completed it.

LIMITING THE CHOICES

Allowing a child to discover and follow his own pattern of mourning is not the same as giving the child license to do whatever he wants. It is easy to feel sorry for the grieving child and consequently relax discipline, standards of acceptable behavior, or expectations. However, loss itself introduces insecurity into the child's world. If his schedule, chores, and what is expected of him also change totally, the child's insecurity is compounded. There is enough uncertainty for the child in exploring the extent of his loss and its meaning in his future; the loss of structure, dependability, rules, and routine brings additional insecurity and should be avoided as much as possible. The line between allowing the freedom to discover and express his own way of grieving, and the abandonment of family discipline, routine, and structure may sometimes be a fine line and a hard one to find. Common sense, coupled with genuine love and acceptance, will generally produce the best responses in an individual situation. Mistakes—if made in the atmosphere of accepting and caring and if admitted by the adult involved—will not do serious harm.

If a child is expected to be present at mealtime, then his freedom to withdraw may be expressed in permission to be silent at the table and to leave as soon as he is finished eating; he should probably still be required to eat his meals with the family. If the child generally goes to bed and gets up at certain times, he should be expected to keep to that schedule. A child should be expected to continue doing his normal duties in the home—making his bed, washing dishes, caring for the dog, doing his homework, practicing the piano. These repeated, expected (although often contested) activities are part of the child's routine; their continuation provides the assurance that life does go on, despite the loss.

In Times of Depression

Some normal activities may become very difficult for the child if his grief is expressed in serious depression. He may find it hard to concentrate on his homework or practice the piano lesson well. Even in this case, I advocate that the activity continue, but perhaps with a reduced amount of time. We may wish to tell the child, "I know that it's hard for you to practice the piano right now. Go ahead and get started, and try to play every piece once. Let me know if it gets to where you just can't go on." We may say, "I realize that you're having a hard time thinking right now. Get started on your homework, and do as much as you can in a half-hour. I'll write a note to your teacher and explain if you don't get it finished." We may offer to stay with him while he practices or does homework.

We can also help the depressed mourner by setting goals and rewarding him when the goals are achieved. These should be simple, short-term objectives, easily within his reach and measurable. For the child old enough to read and write, it may be a list of his daily chores and responsibilities, posted where he can see it and mark off his progress. Loss brings a sense of helplessness and a tendency to feel "What's the use?" or "I can't do anything right anyway." Having visible goals, useful and achievable, lessens the helpless feeling. Seeing the goals accomplished brings satisfaction and the knowledge that "at least I can do that."

Some changes in schedule and routine are inevitable in a loss, especially a major one. There are two ways to make these changes less unsettling and disruptive for a child.

The first is simply to tell the child about the changes. "With the new baby here, you and Tom will have to share a room" or "Since mommy took that new job, you will have to ride the bus to and from school" or "When we move to the new house, you will have to go to a different school." Some changes can be anticipated and prepared for, and these will be discussed in the next chapter. Some are impossible to anticipate and result in piling loss upon loss on a child. Recognizing that multiple losses may intensify and prolong grief will not alleviate the grief, but this can make it more bearable. This situation need not be overwhelming.

If it is possible, allow the child a choice in the changes of schedule and routine, particularly those that affect him most. This can reduce the traumatic effects of the loss. A child should be offered only real choices, not ones that are rigged by decisions already made by others. For example, the child who must give up her room because of a new baby in the family may be allowed to have a part in rearranging or redecorating the room she will now share with a sister. She does not have a choice in surrendering the room, but she can have choices in making the sharing arrangement acceptable and pleasant.

A withdrawn and depressed child will have difficulty making decisions and choices. He needs the reassurance that his feelings are considered and his opinions valued, but his choices should be limited so as not to overwhelm him. Rather than approach the child with the information, "Because of mommy's new job, you will have to give up some of your after-school activities; which ones do you want to drop?" it might be better to limit the choice: "Since mommy has her new job, she can't take you to both swimming and Brownies; would you like to keep on swimming, or would you rather stay in Brownies?"

Setting Time Limits

Another way of limiting the choice is to set a definite time limit. The choice he is making may be for the next week, the next two weeks, or the next month. At the end of that time, the decision will be reexamined, and he will have another opportunity to choose. Part of the difficulty in making choices and decisions while depressed or when mourning is the fear that the choices will turn out "wrong." Loss undermines our self-esteem and self-confidence, and we are less sure of ourselves than normally. A choice involves taking a risk: Maybe we will choose the wrong thing, or we will give up something we really wanted to keep, or we will become committed to something we really dislike. To choose for a limited time period, knowing that the decision is not "forever" and the choice can be reconsidered, decreases the risk.

The depressed child may want to give up all his activities and disengage himself from all his involvements. Limiting his choice to keeping one activity or another tells him that he must continue some of the patterns of his normal life. Just as chores and discipline need to continue throughout the period of grief and mourning, some activities and involvements should be continued. In this way the child begins to learn that life does go on; he eventually rediscovers companionship with friends, enjoyment, and anticipation of the future. The technique of making decisions and choices for a limited time period can also lay for the child the foundation of the one-day-at-a-time approach to life, which is very valuable in future experiences of loss and depression.

THE ANXIOUS CHILD

So far we have been discussing the child who expresses his grief primarily in depression and physical withdrawal from people, places, and activities. Other children seem not to withdraw at all; instead of seeking privacy, they go out of their way to avoid it. They become totally immersed in activities, relationships, and interests. They may be constantly on the move, sleep fitfully and less than usual, and wake up early. This child seems unable to sit still or tolerate silence. If he is alone, the television set is on, the stereo is playing, and he is probably talking on the telephone!

This is an extreme example of another type of withdrawal. This child shields his emotions by becoming so busy and so active that his grief feelings don't have time to "catch up" with him. The parent may be physically near him most of the time, yet have the feeling that the child "isn't really there." The adult may ask himself, "What is he running from?" or "Where has he gone?"

Helping this child may be more difficult and require more active intervention than coping with the depressed person. The child may have us fooled; his activity and interest may look as if he is "all right." Even if his behavior strikes us as a bit forced or frantic, we may tend to shrug it off: "Oh, well, at least he isn't moping around the house!" In fact, the child who is "moping around the house" has a reserve of emotional energy available for the work of mourning that the overinvolved, overactive child does not. The child who protects himself from the pain of grief by building a wall of people, noise, and activity between himself and his feelings may well find his mourning work completed in a distorted fashion, leaving emotional wounds to surface much later.

The Fear of Anger

One possible explanation for the (unconsious) choice of anxiety rather than depression is that the feelings from which the child is hiding are powerful and very frightening. Anger and guilt fit this description; they are both powerful feelings, and anger in particular is very frightening to the child. He fears that his anger may take control of him and fears what he might do when angry. These fears are almost never conscious; the child may not even be aware of the feeling of anger itself. If the child has come to believe that anger is "bad," and if he has learned to be afraid of what he might do while angry, an automatic repression mechanism may be activated as soon as he enters a situation that could be expected to make him angry; the anger is there, but it is not felt or recognized as such.

The angry child needs, most of all, firm, persistent, and physical signs of affection. His anger forms a barrier between him and others that effectively keeps the child from feeling and accepting the love others have for him. Feeling unloved and rejected, the child may himself become rejecting of others; the adults he loves and trusts may be hurt and rebuffed by the child's apparent indifference or his active rejection. Instead of persisting in showing love to the child, the adult may think or say, "If that's the way you want it, have it your own way! If you don't want my love, I'm not going to force it on you!" Yet this may be precisely what the child needs: Physical expressions of love "forced" upon him, breaking down the barrier he has put up, and finally reaching him. The child needs to feel and learn, by our attitudes and actions, "There's nothing you can do to make me stop loving you. You may act as hateful, angry, and irritable as you like, but I still love you, and I intend to go on loving you!"

If the child is small enough for the adult to pick him up and hold him tightly, this is one good way of responding to the angry child. He may struggle and fight against the embrace for a while; the adult may need to continue to hold him firmly and envelop him. When Jimmy was so anxious, irritable, and downright obnoxious after John Hillis died, I was finally able to comfort him after I went to his room, picked him up, and insisted that he hug me as tightly as he could. This was not done without a struggle; Jimmy acted as if he wanted me to put him down and leave him alone. As I held him, I told him, "I'll let you go just as soon as you give me a good, tight hug." When Jimmy finally hugged me tightly, he began to relax and to cry. Then he was able to accept my comfort and my presence—something he had wanted all along, but was unable to accept because of his anger.

Another effective way that I deal with Jimmy when he is angry is to wrestle with him on the floor or to tickle him until he begs me to stop. Both means give him the comfort of physical contact and help break down the barriers that ward off my love. The child who is too big to pick up and hold in a struggle may nevertheless be tickled or wrestled. I personally won't let Jimmy box with me or get involved in physical expressions of anger that could hurt me or himself. Other alternatives for physical contact with the angry child include touch football, dancing, or arm-wrestling.

Staying in Control

Part of a child's fear of his anger is the danger of losing control. He needs the reassurance of an adult who is able to control the situation and also control the child physically if necessary. For this reason, I believe that our choice of physical expressions of love and physical contact with the angry child should be limited to activities in which we are able to retain control and in which no one will be injured.

The child who is expressing his grief in anger or anxiety is physically restless. Physiologically his body is geared for action. By himself, however, the child is incapable of sustained activity; his pacing is aimless; he begins one thing after another, without completing any. An adult can help this child expend his nervous energy by providing the sustaining force to carry through the physical activity. If the child is pacing, the adult may take him outside for a twenty-or-thirty-minute walk, keeping up a brisk pace and refusing to allow the child to stop midway. If the child begins shooting baskets, the adult may join him and continue the game for twenty minutes or a half-hour. Riding a bicycle, running, jumping rope, and dancing (try thirty minutes of polka!) are all good physical outlets for anger and anxiety. If the physical activity is continued for twenty or thirty minutes at a vigorous level, it will help to relax the child and release some inner tension.

The relaxation that comes after vigorous physical activity is a good time for the adult to show his love for the child in quieter but still physical ways. A good way is to hold the child and rock him, rub his back, or just sit quietly close to him with an arm around him or holding his hand.

Accepting a child's feelings does not mean accepting every way he chooses to express those feelings. The angry child in particular is aware that there are accepted and unaccepted ways of behaving in the family; in his fear of losing control of the situation he may deliberately test the adult's control of the situation by acting in ways that he knows are unacceptable. Our refusal to set limits on his behavior at times like this can increase his insecurity and make him afraid that we, too, are unable to control the situation and, especially, control him.

The angry child may have even more need for firm discipline and a dependable schedule than the child whose grief takes the form of depression. In schedule, routine, and activities, his need will be less that of motivating him to continue his activities than of insisting he follow through on what he begins. This child may need our help in limiting his activities and slowing him down, rather than (as with the depressed child) our encouragement to try something new.

The guidelines for limiting choices hold true for the angry or anxious child as well as for the depressed. The angry person also has difficulty with choices and decisions; he, too, should be faced with limited options. For him, too, the one-day-at-a-time approach is helpful and valid.

Identifying Anger

The angry child is easy to identify once we are aware of anger as one of the feelings of grief and begin to look for this reaction. The child's "body language" shouts at us, our own bodies respond, and the combination of his body language and our physical reactions should tell us accurately when we are dealing with an angry child. The child will be rigid and tense, with a set facial expression—often a scowl or a frown. He is easily offended, irritable, nervous. He seems to be in constant motion, unable to settle down.

Our physical reactions to him are those of defensiveness and tension. We may feel a tightening of the neck and shoulder muscles (the child is a literal "pain in the neck"!). We may get a headache. We may have a "knot" in the pit of our stomach. We will generally be able to recognize readily our own feelings of hostility, avoidance, and defensiveness in the presence of the angry child. Our behavior toward him will confirm these feelings; it will tend to be abrupt, demanding, authoritarian, impatient. Of course, we may be angry or anxious ourselves over matters that have nothing to do with the child, and we may thus "take it out" on the child unwisely. However, if we are not under any particular stress and yet find our entire mood and behavior change when we are around the child, this is a clue that we may be dealing with an angry child.

The child under eight or nine tends to express his anger and anxiety physically by his posture, expression, and violent and sudden movements. Older children, who are beginning to gain some mastery over the world intellectually, may express their anger in more rational ways. As they learn to gain control in their world by means of understanding, so too they may seek to control a loss situation by attempting to understand what happened.

The child eight to twelve may genuinely need answers to questions regarding why the loss occurred and what happened. An understanding of the circumstances of the loss may be genuinely helpful. However, this child may also use endless questions, particularly those expressing or implying blame, as a means of expressing anger or frustration. In some cases we find that every time we are able to answer a child's question, he comes back with two or three more. Every time we attempt to moderate his blame of something or someone as a cause for his loss, he raises a multitude of new objections. We find ourselves becoming angry and frustrated in trying to answer the child's questions. We want to say, "Go away, and don't bother me with your questions anymore!" Or else we find ourselves avoiding the child and becoming "too busy to talk" when he approaches us.

110

Responding on an Emotional Level

Anger is an emotion. Calm, logical answers to his questions, and reasons for what has happened, reach the child on the intellectual but not the emotional level. Although many or all of a child's questions need to be answered eventually, the first step is to deal with his anger. One effective way of approaching the feelings underlying the questions and blame is to respond to the emotion that seems to lie beneath the questions, and not the questions themselves. Using the evidences of "body language"—both our own and the child's—it should not be too difficult to identify the child whose questions represent anger. We might respond to this child with a statement like "It sounds as if you are feeling frustrated and confused" or "This really is a tough time for you; I wonder if you are feeling upset and hurt." I would avoid saying the word *anger* in confronting the child with his probable feelings, especially the child of seven or older. He may not recognize that he is angry; moreover, he may view anger as a "taboo" feeling, not generally accepted as okay in society. The child under seven may respond easily and naturally to a statement such as "I think you might be feeling angry" or "This has been a tough time; I wonder if it makes you mad." The older child might feel that this implies there is something wrong with him and respond with defensiveness, hostility, and withdrawal.

It is also important that we phrase our statements so that the child realizes we are stating our own opinions and observations. He should feel free to agree with our impressions or to correct them. It is less likely to make the child defensive and withdrawn to say, "I think you might be feeling. . . ," than to say, "You are. . . ." The latter implies that we have already passed judgment on the child and his feelings; it is less likely to give him the impression that we are ready to hear what he thinks and feels.

Once we have asked the child about his feelings and given him the implicit permission both to feel and express them, he may be ready to admit, "Yes, I'm really mad!" or "I'm feeling so angry, I don't know what to do!" Again, this is the child who needs extra and obvious expressions of our love and acceptance.

An approach that allows the child to "get in touch" with his feelings—which basically gives him "permission" to feel what he is feeling—might result in a storm of tears or an outbreak of anger.

This will probably be uncomfortable and might even make us feel guilty for "upsetting" the child. Grief is emotional, however, and emotions can rarely be handled satisfactorily in an unemotional manner. A calm, rational discussion of feelings generally does not provide the release and healing the child needs; this is more likely to come after a storm of tears, a period of angry shouting and pacing, or a time of pounding furiously on the bed.

Limits on Behavior

Permission for a child to express his angry feelings is not license to do just anything at all that he feels like doing. It is important for both the adult and the child to have the limits of acceptable behavior clearly understood and firmly enforced. For example, a child may be allowed to stamp angrily up the stairs to his room, but slamming the door may be forbidden. In general, any expression of anger that carries the risk of physical harm to the child or someone else, or which is destructive of property, should be off limits. Punching bags, beds, chairs, and sofas (and maybe the floor) may be pounded in the child's fury; he may not hit his sister, kick the dog, or throw dishes.

Even the child's verbal expressions of frustration and anger should have limits. Although I allow my children to shout, "I hate you!" at me, this is not acceptable in some households. It is probably more accurate and more acceptable to ask the child to say, "I'm so furious with you!" or "I'm very angry with you!" As he gets older, he should be taught to express his feelings precisely in the terms "I feel . . ." rather than using statements such as, "You make me so mad!" or "You never listen to me!" or "You always say no to what I want!" It helps the child to recognize the emotion as his own and minimizes his natural tendency to blame others for what he feels and what happens to him.

There may also be limits on the expressions of other feelings. Just because a child doesn't *feel* like doing anything is no reason *not* to do anything. The child will feel more comfortable with his feelings as he learns that he doesn't need to be their slave; as he learns this, it is the parent or other adult he loves and trusts who helps him distinguish between what he feels and what he does about it. These are the aspects in which the adult can help the child by maintaining a firm, caring control on the child's actions while still exhibiting an acceptance of his feelings. Most parents (and other adults dealing with children) are probably familiar with the phrase "You don't have to like it; you just have to do it!"

One aspect of a child's grief behavior that can cause great concern is a change in sleeping and eating patterns. It is worrisome to us when a child doesn't eat or we're afraid he isn't getting enough sleep. As a rule, these problems resolve spontaneously as the child accomplishes his mourning work, and they do not usually need specific intervention by the parent. In fact, it is better not to make an issue of eating; let him eat as he is able. The child should be expected to adhere to family mealtimes; if he is eating much less than normal, we can add a couple of regular snack times during the day. In dealing with the child's feelings, we are approaching the issue of eating and sleeping behavior at its root. The child who does not recover his appetite within several weeks, or who loses a lot of weight, may need special counseling. And, of course, a child who has diabetes or some other illness for which diet is important needs more attention in his eating habits.

In most cases of childhood grief, I strongly oppose sleeping pills and tranquilizers. Physical activity, back rubs, hot baths, soft music, and quiet companionship are much more natural ways to release anxiety and tension and don't interfere with the unconscious aspects of mourning. Sleeping pills interfere with the dream process, and dreaming is an important tool of our unconscious for solving problems and bringing healing.

FEELING GUILTY

Anger and guilt are very closely related emotions. In grief and mourning, they are so closely intertwined as to be almost indistinguishable. Anger can be expressed as blame of others, or it may turn inward and result in feelings of guilt. Instead of an either-or situation, particularly in the grief process, there is usually some combination of the two. There is simultaneously the expression of anger, in blaming others for the loss the child has suffered, and the deep feeling of guilt, as he blames himself in some way. In the search for reasons for the loss, for an explanation for his feelings of grief, the child is almost compelled to find someone to blame— either himself or someone else or a combination of these. In any loss situation, guilt is a common feeling.

113

Guilt accompanies feelings of anger because in our social climate, anger is usually considered a "bad" feeling. The child is given many verbal and nonverbal messages that he "should not" feel angry. If he recognizes feelings of anger, he may feel guilty about them. If the anger is directed toward God or toward adults he loves and trusts, particularly parents, guilt is even more likely to be present. His parents are "doing what is best"; they love him and care for him; it is "wrong" to be angry with them for what they do or what they allow to happen. Feelings toward God are even more intense. God is all-knowing and all-good; what He does, what He allows to happen, must be right and good. In the child's view, if he is angry with God, there must be something wrong with him; the alternative is that there is something wrong with God, and that is impossible!

Grief over the loss of a person who is important to the child also includes a measure of rejection. If the child is rejected by someone older, wiser, and "better" than he, then again, the fault must lie with the child; he must have done something, thought something, or said something wrong.

Guilt in children is difficult to handle. It is often a mixture of feelings of guilt over imagined misdoings and feelings over actual errors and faults. From birth to adolescence and beyond, the child is continually blamed for his part in various loss situations. Whether it is a homework assignment, a new jacket, a library book, or lunch money, the child is immediately accused (or at least, feels accused) of being to blame for the loss. In many cases the child *is* to blame. He has a short attention span and a selective memory; things that are important to the adults in his life do not have the same significance to him; he may have forgotten, mislaid, or ignored, resulting in the loss. Consequently a link is made in the child's emotional being between the feelings of grief and the feelings of guilt, and the grief often triggers guilt.

Uncertain Influence

The child also has only a vague idea of the limitations of his control of and responsibility for what happens in his world. The two-to-five-year-old still lives in a world in which ideas, abstract concepts, and natural forces are personified. He relates to them the same way he relates to people; his influence over them is the same as his influence over people in his world. Because he can influence and sometimes manipulate people in his world by his expressed or even unexpressed thoughts and wishes, he is unable to grasp the fact that ideas, abstract concepts, and the forces of nature are not subject to his control by wishing or thinking. If he has thought "bad" thoughts, maybe these "bad" thoughts were the cause of something "bad" that happened. If he can wish for a bicycle and find it in the garage on his birthday or under the tree on Christmas morning, maybe his wish that daddy would go away, that mommy would get sick, or that his baby brother would die was the cause of illness or injury.

A child gradually comes to learn that his thoughts and wishes do not in themselves have the power to harm anyone—unless he acts deliberately and directly to make them come true. Yet the sneaking suspicion that dislike or anger really can harm someone else lingers all the way into adulthood, though lessening in intensity with coming to maturity. The small child faces a paradox between the realization of his smallness and weakness and his sense of great importance and power. As the center of his universe, he is bound to feel guilt and responsibility over the loss of something important to him, even the death of someone he loves.

Expressing Guilt

It is not easy for a child to express his feelings of guilt. He may find them too shameful and too private to share. If an adult suspects the child may be feeling guilt, he may be able to broach the subject and help the child to verbalize his guilt by sharing his own feelings: "You know, Johnny, I've been sorry many times that I didn't stop at grandma's house the morning before she died. She called and asked me to come over, but I was very busy that day and told her I'd come over later in the week" or "I've been sorry ever since Aunt Mabel died that I didn't call her on the telephone that Sunday and tell her that I loved her and was thinking of her."

As with anger, guilt feelings must be dealt with first on the emotional, not intellectual, level. The child may need a "confessor" to whom he can reveal the extent of his guilt and from whom he can receive some assurance of forgiveness. This "confessor" may be a parent, a close adult friend, a priest or pastor; the important thing is that the child feels free to talk about his guilt, and the adult is wise enough to listen. In the Christian home, the child may be asked to turn to God with his confession of his guilt, anger, ill-wishes, or behavior. The "confessor" can then reassure the child of God's acceptance, forgiveness, and love.

Once the child is relieved of the guilt feelings through confession and the assurance of forgiveness, it may be important to help him understand that he did not make daddy go away, cause mommy's illness, or cause his little sister's accident. If the child feels guilt in relation to someone still living, he may find release in telephoning, visiting, or writing that person to "confess" and ask forgiveness. If his guilt relates to one who has died, an adult may need to reassure the child that he has the forgiveness of the person he has "wronged." His understanding that his thoughts and actions did not cause illness or death is probably best accomplished by a simple, brief explanation of the real causes.

Whether the guilt is real or imagined, it seems real to the child. For this reason it is good to deal with it in terms of confession and forgiveness first. If the question of whether the child is really guilty still needs to be settled in his mind, this should be done after the process of confession and forgiveness.

As stated before, these guidelines are necessarily broad and general. Probably no child's grief situation is completely covered by these suggestions. But this discussion should prove helpful in understanding the needs of the grieving child and seeing the options for responding to these needs. Yet an adult's best allies for coping with a child's grief, and helping that child to cope with it, are a love and acceptance of the child, an ability to listen to him, and one's own common sense.

6 / HELPING A CHILD TO MOURN

THE TASKS OF MOURNING are the steps a child takes, consciously or unconsciously, to move from the "before" way of life to the "after." The mourning period is the time during which the child negotiates the transition between normal life before his loss and the new normal life that emerges as he discovers the extent of the loss, finds its meaning in terms of his daily life, and makes the adjustments necessary to live without it. The steps include testing the reality of the loss; discovering the numerous intangible losses involved; "letting go" of what was lost by accepting its absence; compiling and completing a memory of the loss; and recovering the emotional energy needed for new relationships and activities. This mourning is, by our definition, the psychological work that accompanies the complex of feelings that constitute grief.

This chapter focuses on the ways parents and other significant adults can help a child negotiate the changes in everyday life wrought by the loss. In general we will be discussing "bridge-building" techniques—ways to help the child bridge the gap between the "before" and the "after." Just as the previous chapter presented various ways of responding to the grief feelings, so this discussion will offer various ways of helping the child to mourn —to make the transition from old to new.

THE MENTOR RELATIONSHIP

The mentor relationship is a good starting point, for it parallels many aspects of the emotional process of moving through the various tasks of mourning.

There is initially an intense involvement between the child and the mentor. The child's time and attention are almost completely taken up with the relationship; he talks, thinks, and dreams about his mentor; he spends as much time as possible with him; he copies the mentor's mannerisms, walk, dress, and ideas. He patterns his behavior according to what his mentor would think of it, seeking to do things the mentor approves and avoiding the disapproved. Little discrimination or judgment is exercised; in the child's eyes the mentor is perfect, his word is law, his decisions right and final.

After a while, the involvement with the mentor becomes less intense. The child is no longer totally involved in the relationship. He begins to think and talk about other things, notice other people, and become involved in activities that do not relate to the mentor relationship. He also imitates the mentor less faithfully. The child begins to exercise some judgment, dares to disagree, and sees that the mentor is not perfect or the final authority on everything.

Eventually there is a change in the quality of the child–mentor relationship. Parts of the mentor have been internalized by the child—ideas, habits, interests, mannerisms—have become truly his own, expressed in individual and personal ways. Parts of the mentor have been discarded as not fitting the child's personality and individuality. The time of intense identification with the mentor becomes a part of the child's memory; this vivid picture tends to remain lifelong and is generally viewed with affection and appreciation. But because the intense emotional involvement has ceased, the child's energy is free to turn to other interests and relationships.

There are mentor relationships that do not move into a phase of natural ending, of course. If the child adopts a parent or grandparent as a mentor, the quality of the relationship may continue through much of life. There are instances in which an adolescent forms a mentor relationship with an older person of the opposite sex whom he or she eventually marries; the mentor relationship may form a part of the marriage for years, even for life. However, most of the mentor relationships of preadolescent children follow the pattern to a natural ending.

Parallels to Loss

After a loss, a child may exhibit some or all of the same types of behavior as in a mentor relationship. He may spend a lot of time talking and thinking about what has been lost. There may be a

118

period of intense identification. What was lost may be idolized and idealized; the child may be unable to exercise judgment or discrimination regarding the lost person, place, or circumstances and may view it as "practically perfect in every way."

Gradually the identification becomes internalized. Parts of it are discarded, and what is kept is adapted to the child's own growing personality and present circumstances. In time, his view of what he lost becomes more objective; he dares to criticize it and becomes able to tolerate criticism of it by others. He is able to see the lost thing in realistic terms rather than as all "good" or all "bad." There is also a feeling of relief. During this time, what was lost has become a memory for the child—a memory that may be vivid, often affectionate, but also involving his active emotions and energy. Recovery from grief does not mean that the child has "forgotten" what he lost; it generally means that he has accepted that the lost thing has a place in his past, but except as a memory, not in his present or future. The decisions and activities of daily living are no longer based on "What would grandpa think?" or "How would we do this back home?"

The timetable for this work of mourning varies greatly, depending on the age of the child, his emotional development, his involvement with the thing lost, other circumstances of life—especially other losses—and the nature of the loss itself. Some losses bring a return to mourning work over a long period of time; as the child grows and matures, he may need to mourn these newly discovered aspects of an old loss. This may be particularly true in the case of the loss of a parent or a home, community, or church early in life. Returning to the work of mourning long after the loss does not necessarily indicate distorted mourning or an inadequate dealing with the loss earlier. It may merely denote the child's maturing personality and understanding and, with this, uncovering aspects of loss he could not appreciate at the time it occurred.

"LITTLE DEATHS"

"Little deaths," as already described, include a wide range of usually minor losses. Though they may not be insignificant—representing true loss and real grief—they are nonetheless "little." The child's attachment to and emotional investment in the various objects lost in these "little deaths" are limited. These losses tend to be associated with very few areas of life and disrupt it little.

For example, Juanita's headband was a limited loss. It was only a part of her memory of our trip to Dallas; it figured to a limited degree in the way she saw herself; she had not spent a lot of time and energy dreaming about, planning for, and wishing to own the headband, and her emotional involvement in it was not great; her daily routine was not really affected by this loss, nor was her sense of security.

There was a short period of time after losing the headband when Juanita talked and thought about it and wanted to replace it. She reviewed the memory of the shopping trip during which she bought it; she commented on the clothes she could have worn with it; she spent time trying on other headbands from the same set.

But within a couple of days, she had "let go" of the headband. She no longer spent a lot of time talking about it; she stopped asking for a replacement. Yet she has not forgotten it; even three years later she remembered it with pleasure and mentioned it.

In the event of a limited "little death" like Juanita's loss of the headband, the role of the parent or other involved adult is generally that of a supportive bystander. The child will be able to work through the loss and accomplish the work of mourning himself. The adult may need to do no more than help the child realize the fact of the loss and permit him to grieve over it. The adult may share in the child's memories of what was lost and join in "remember" talks.

Even so, "little deaths" are generally more complex than they seem at first and perhaps more complex than we adults recognize. They will require a certain amount of mourning for the child to be able to "let go" of the loss and restructure his life without it. They may also involve some degree of the child's identity and self-image and therefore require time for adjustment—as in the loss of Jimmy's wallet.

The Loss of "Blankey"

One "little death" that requires special consideration is the loss of the "blankey." This loss is neither small nor insignificant to the child; it is almost equivalent to losing an arm or leg. The "blankey" *is* a part of the child; its loss will require adequate mourning. Because this child is generally aged two or three, the grief and mourning will be primarily unconscious. They may also be accomplished relatively easily, within only a few days.

The parent or other involved adult may assist the work of mourning in this case in several ways. The child will need physical comfort and time to adjust to the absence of "blankey" and the loss of identity and security involved. Evidences of grief may be seen in the child's regressing (wetting pants or bed, using baby talk) or in clinging more to parents. He may ask to be held, to be carried, to sleep with mommy and daddy.

Extra hugs and kisses, permission to behave "like a baby" instead of "like a big boy" for a while in some ways, and providing a physical presence are some ways of helping the child handle the loss. The child will generally tend to abandon his clinging behavior and regression spontaneously once the unconscious process of mourning is completed.

As in other aspects of helping a child cope with loss, the attitude of the adult is at least as important as what he says or does. A firm, affectionate, but rather matter-of-fact approach is my own choice. The adult should be available if the child needs and wants him, but should not force attention on the child (except in dealing with anger, as previously noted). The child needs assurance that the adult has confidence in him, believes in his ability to deal with the crisis, and knows that the crisis won't last forever.

The development of emotional skills in a child is similar to the development of physical skills. There is a time to let go of the child's hand when he is learning to walk, a time to wait for him to pick himself up when he falls, and a time to take the training wheels off the bicycle. In learning to negotiate the tasks of mourning, the child also comes to a point at which the parent needs to allow him to "pick himself up when he falls."

Overconcern, overprotectiveness, and overreadiness to offer advice may instill in the child a fear that he will not be able to cope, that he has been hurt worse than he knows. By its nature, loss produces some insecurity; a marked change in the behavior of the adults in his life may further threaten his security. An adult's overall discipline and expectations should not change greatly during the mourning period; "permission" to regress should be limited to only a few aspects of the routine.

Older Children's Losses

There are losses suffered by the older child that may correspond to the loss of the "blankey." The loss of objects that the child identifies closely with himself and his security is also, in effect, a loss of a part of himself—a beloved doll, a stuffed animal, a favorite article of clothing, or even a piece of furniture. If the child's grief seems out of proportion to the object lost, it is wise to remember that the loss and grief suffered are defined by the child, not an adult. The fact is, the grief may not be out of proportion to the loss, but rather, the loss is more significant than we realized.

SCHOOLS AND LOSS

In the event of the loss of a place, a context in which the child sees himself, much the same process can be observed. One of the natural, expected losses of context is a child's promotion from one grade to another in the same school. Initially there is a time of comparing the new classroom with the former, the new teacher with the previous one, differences in the surroundings such as the location of doors and windows, pencil sharpeners, and bookcases. There is contrast in the daily routine, recess time, lunch time, and classroom rules. For the first week or more, the child will be orienting himself to the new classroom, new schedule, and new identity as a fourth-grader, not a third-grader.

Most of these changes and adaptations come quickly, easily, and unconsciously. Neither child nor parent nor teacher would identify them as "mourning." We call it "learning our way around" and accept it as a normal part of change. However, the same "learning our way around" is part of the work of mourning any loss. Indeed, it is discovering the meaning of the loss and the changes it brings.

Changing Grades

Many elements in changing grades, even within the same school, parallel the tasks of mourning. The child "loses" his old classroom, his former teacher, his previous routine, and his former identity. During the first few weeks of school he discovers the extent of the changes; he "lets go" his former desk, room, teacher, and identity during the summer and at the start of the new school year.

There are a number of "helps" built into the process of changing grades. The change is expected and prepared for during the school year. The fourth-grader is told from time to time, "When you are in fifth grade you will study this." The second-grader is reminded, "You'll need to know this next year in third grade." The child has an opportunity to see and visit other classrooms in the school; he will change to a room he has seen before, not a totally unfamiliar one. There are also class pictures, a yearbook, and other reminders of the previous year. There are ritual events that mark the ending of school; a time for goodbys and reliving some events with classmates; school picnics, field day, school plays, recitals, talent shows, and closing ceremonies.

The fact of loss and the feelings of grief are balanced by the pride of promotion to another grade, the anticipation of learning new things, the excitement of being a year older. Along with the loss, the child experiences much obvious gain in new privileges and responsibilities. There is also the interval of the summer vacation—time to make the transition from being a second-grader to being a third-grader. The child does not lose one role, one schedule, one identity and move immediately into another; summer vacation helps him negotiate the passage.

Another advantage for the child who is changing grades is the fact that many things stay the same. The school building is familiar; many teachers and administrators return; most classmates and companions make the change with him, so he remains part of the same group.

Changing Schools

The child who changes schools, especially in the middle of the year, tends to feel his loss and grief more acutely. He experiences a larger number of losses and has fewer of the supports that are built into promotion to a higher grade. In contrast with the total complex of end-of-the-year activities that ritualize the promotion, the child may have no ceremony or ritual to mark his change of schools. At most the ceremony may be a single farewell party squeezed into the last half-hour of a normal school day. His loss includes familiar schoolrooms, buildings, and grounds; the schedule and routine; the security of knowing staff and teachers; the companionship of classmates. If the change comes while school is in session, and not over a vacation break, there is no time interval in which to negotiate the change, feel his grief, and accomplish his work of mourning. The child abruptly ceases to be a student at one school and immediately begins to be a student at another.

Since midterm changes in school are often the result of a family move, a change in financial position, or a divorce or death in the family, the child may also be dealing with other forms of loss. Thus the grief is compounded. There may also be fewer and less obvious gains.

As a result, evidences of mourning work may be more obvious in this child. He may insist on wearing a school T-shirt or jacket from his "old" school during his first days or weeks in the new one. He may spend much time comparing his previous schoolroom, playgrounds, teachers, principal, schedule, and companions with the new. He may be quick to let people know that he "just transferred into Theodore Roosevelt from Sipp School." He may copy styles of dress and mannerisms of his former companions and classmates to an exaggerated degree; he may complain about the way things are done at Theodore Roosevelt in contrast to Sipp. In short, the child may go through a period of intense identification with his former school. This may also be a time of idealization of Sipp School as Utopia.

In time, the child begins to think of himself as a Theodore Roosevelt student instead of a Sipp student. The references to Sipp in his conversation become less frequent; he begins to notice and appreciate special aspects of Theodore Roosevelt and recall ways in which Sipp was less than perfect. As this happens, the child is able to make deeper commitments and form deeper attachments in his new school—new friends, extracurricular activities, and, in general, "settle in." The child may even exchange his Sipp T-shirt or jacket for a Theodore Roosevelt!

Eventually the child's view of the change in schools becomes more balanced. He is able to realize and admit what he lost, but he also can accept the loss and recognize the gains. Finally the child has a memory of Sipp that remains part of his past and his past identity, but that leaves him free to accept and live his new identity.

Negative Identification

Identification with the thing lost—in this case a school—may be totally opposite to what I have described. Instead of idealizing Sipp School as Utopia, the child may idealize Theodore Roosevelt and act as though the school change was the best thing that ever happened to him! Although his conversation is still intensely involved with Sipp School, his comments will be negative and derogatory. He may seem to remember nothing at all good about Sipp, yet his attention and emotional energy are still totally involved there. Everything at Theodore Roosevelt seems infinitely better than anything at Sipp: teachers, schedule, rooms, cafeteria, playgrounds, even the color of the chalkboards and the location of the drinking fountains.

Negative identification may be more intense than its opposite and may last longer. The child may unconsciously adopt a negative attitude to shield himself from the painful grief of the loss; in effect, the child tells himself, "I really didn't lose much of anything. Things are much better now. There's really nothing to feel sad or cry about." The relief feelings are strong and even exaggerated, whereas most of the other aspects of grief feelings are denied, repressed, or deferred.

Strong feelings of anger may accompany negative identification. The anger is expressed, in this instance, in a "safe" and acceptable form, for it appears that the child is making a good adjustment to the change and is happy in his new circumstances. But adults should keep in mind the more subtle expressions of anger and the means of identifying and handling them, as discussed in chapter 5.

The child who makes a negative identification with that which he lost may eventually have to admit to himself that his loss really was painful and does entail grief. This may come as a surprise to the parents. Suddenly—days or weeks after the change in schools—the pain of the child's grief begins to appear—after an apparently smooth and painless acceptance and adjustment.

Whether or not the child exhibits grief behavior, his work of mourning in the event of negative identification proceeds as a mirror-image to that of positive identification. In this case, the child reaches a point where he is able to recall positive things about his old school; he may wear his Sipp T-shirt or jacket again; he will speak less of comparisons between the two schools; he will eventually come to a balanced picture, accepting both the gains and the losses he has experienced as a result of the change; he will recognize a past identity as a Sipp student. The child may also move to a positive identification at that point.

Emotional Energy

The emotional energy involved in a negative relationship or negative identification is probably stronger and more intense than their positive counterparts. (It seems to require more energy to hate than to love.) Even though the child whose identification with Sipp School is negative may plunge headlong into activities at Theodore Roosevelt, he will not have the emotional energy free to make deep commitments or attachments at Theodore Roosevelt until he has completed his mourning work. Relationships and involvements will tend to be superficial as long as a large amount of the child's emotional energy is involved with Sipp School, even though the involvement is negative. When the mourning work is completed, there may well be a noticeable change in the quality of the child's involvement in activities and relationships in the new school. He may exhibit a more relaxed, less intense attitude and a deeper commitment to them.

Preparing for Change

There are various ways in which adults can help a child cope with a change of school. Some of these are not inherently different from ways to cope with other kinds of loss.

If possible, the child should be prepared for the change in advance, even if the preparation involves only a few days or weeks. He can be told, "When you start going to your new school . . . ," and some of the expected changes can be discussed. We may offer him a chance to think and talk about some of the potential changes. It may be possible for the child to visit the new school, meet his new teacher and some new classmates, before actually attending. If a visit is unfeasible, pictures of the school or last year's yearbook may be obtained.

Again, if possible, it may be wise to introduce a "vacation" at the time the change is made. Even if it means keeping the child out of school for a week or so, it provides a little time to "give up" all that he is losing and, in a sense, to "shift gears" to be ready to attend the new school. A classroom farewell and possibly even a farewell party at home with nonschool friends can help by providing a degree of ceremony to mark the ending. It may also be possible to arrange for a "welcome party" in the new classroom during the first week there.

The child should be encouraged to exchange school pictures with friends, teachers, perhaps the principal, and other "special" people in the old school. An address and autograph book provides the possibility of contacting special friends in the future. Whether or not the addresses and phone numbers are ever used, they provide the security of a link to parts of the past. If the child has the ability to contact friends from the former school, the decision to complete the break and give up the contact lies with him; this gives him a measure of control over the loss and tends to decrease any sense of helplessness and frustration.

The parent may suggest that the child make a scrapbook of his old school and assist him with it. Photographs of friends, the buildings, the classroom, parties, and special events may be included; also, school newsletters or memos, completed school work, even pressed leaves from trees in the playground. Even if the child resists the idea of keeping any mementos of the old school, the parent may wish to keep a few reminders for future reference. Depending on the child's own way of coping with the loss, his readiness to deal with reminders of the school and to compile a memory may come early or late in the mourning process. In most situations, there is some point during the mourning period when the child will want and appreciate tangible reminders of the loss.

It may be possible to provide other links with the old school during the time of adjustment. These include a return visit to the school, perhaps in time for end-of-the-year activities; arranging to receive the school newspaper or student publication temporarily if there is one; or perhaps having a special friend from his former school come for a visit if this is geographically practical.

MOVING AWAY

These same suggestions are useful in the event of a family move across town, across the country, or overseas. In general, such moves incur grief in proportion to the "distance" between the old home and the new; the fewer the things that remain the same after the move, the greater the child's grief is likely to be.

Changes in location are much more important to a child five

years old and over than to someone younger. The emotional energy of the child under five is usually absorbed in himself and his own body; his physical context is limited to a few important people and some significant surroundings such as toys, blankets, and clothes. The loss of a room, a home, or a neighborhood will not have a great deal of impact on him as long as the important people remain in their familiar places and the objects to which he is attached move with him.

Loss of location and context begins to bring grief when a child begins to move into the outside world, forming relationships outside his family and interacting with the community beyond his own front door. This varies for each person, but can usually be expected to begin at about the time a child enters school.

The Temporary Move

In one type of loss of context, a child may seem to deny the loss successfully and appear to need no time for mourning: A move perceived as temporary. This could characterize the missionary child on furlough, the child of a business executive transferred overseas for a year or two, or the child whose parents accept a short-term business assignment involving a move. For this child, the place he has left retains its identity as home. He may never make a break with his home and may never form a significant attachment to his temporary new location.

In terms of the mourning process, this child appears to remain at the point of intense identification with the home he has left and to which he expects to return. He may idealize the home setting, spending much time and emotional energy in thinking, talking, and dreaming of "home." The child may spend the entire period of time in the new location with a sense of detachment and unreality, as if he were only partly there. He may seem to be in a state of suspension, waiting to begin "life" again when he gets home. Even so, there is an unconscious separation from "home" and some degree of unconscious attachment to the new environment.

When the family does return home, both the child and the setting will have changed. Time has not stood still; the child is different, and his place in his home environment has not remained as it was when he vacated it. Upon his return the child may perform a dual task of mourning: Mourning for the "home" he left temporarily, and mourning for the location that was his temporary home. He may also show a fierce, unexpected attachment to the place and circumstances which were his temporary home—a grief that seems all out of proportion to his attitudes and expressed opinions while he actually was there.

Children who experience the loss of context through repeated temporary dislocations may accumulate a backlog of grief and respond to some single loss with the pent-up grief and deferred mourning of many past losses. The responses can also be seen in the child who experiences several or successive other kinds of losses that are perceived as temporary in nature.

Any loss that is expected to be temporary is more difficult to mourn than one perceived and accepted as permanent. However, even temporary losses tend to bring with them some permanent losses, usually intangibles. In the case of the child who moves temporarily from his hometown, life goes on and the child continues to grow and develop during the time of the temporary loss. Such temporary losses as a broken arm or leg can entail permanent intangible losses, such as a missed season on the football team. Children who have suffered a number of serious losses in quick succession, or who have accumulated a backlog of grief and deferred mourning because of repeated "temporary" losses, may benefit from professional help.

PART OF A GROUP

Another source of help to a mourning child is the ability to identify with someone else who has suffered the same experience or loss. John Harris was helped in dealing with being a "boy without a daddy" by finding that there were two children he knew in his school who were without a mommy. For the child whose family is constantly on the move, particularly in a "back-and-forth" fashion, the losses are somewhat easier to bear if they are accepted as part of a lifestyle that is shared by friends and acquaintances. The child of missionary parents expects to return to the United States from the mission field for one year of every four or five. His identity is that of an "M.K." or "missionary's kid"; this includes his identity of "being from" the United States while living in Ecuador and "being from" Ecuador while on furlough in the U.S. The child's identity as an M.K. may figure largely in his total concept of himself; it gives him a group to which he belongs, a community in which he is accepted and understood. An M.K. from Africa and an M.K. from Brazil may identify more readily with each other than either of them does with other children of American parents or with other children native to the country of service.

Part of the child's distress included in the loss of identity is the feeling that he is different from others, excluded from "the group," and alone. The feeling of aloneness and isolation, of being different and excluded, is a common part of many losses. Finding another person or a group of people who are "just like" him in the nature of the loss can boost self-confidence. It can open up choices in the way he handles the loss, and it can help him feel more normal and acceptable. The pain and terror of isolation is diminished or completely dispelled as he becomes able to identify himself as part of a special group. This fact holds true for adults as well and underlies the success of support groups such as Divorce Recovery, Parents Without Partners, Widows Involved Together, Make Today Count, and others.

A child can be helped in several ways to find an identity as part of a group. The example of another child in the class who changed schools in the middle of the year; the example of a Ted Kennedy, Jr., who suffered the loss of a leg; the example of a Joni Eareckson, who became a quadriplegic; the example of the neighbor child whose parents are divorced; the cousin whose father was killed in an automobile accident—all these can be pointed out to the child. Examples of "ordinary" children, in many respects "just like you," tend to be more useful than examples of "heroes," or children who are set apart from the crowd by special status or talent. Anecdotes from the parents' own past may also be useful. However, the child may approach parents or "heroes" as if they were "larger than life," with an attitude of awe that makes identification less complete. The example that is likely to help the child most is one to which he can respond, "Hey, he's just like me!"

Examples From Books

Another source of examples for identification is books, either biography or fiction. A good fictional representation of a believable character dealing with realistic loss situations can be very helpful.

There is an increasing volume of children's fiction in which the main theme of the book revolves around a major loss in a child's life and the ways the child deals with it. Many of these books deal positively and realistically with feelings, behavior, doubts, fears, victories, and defeats for the child in handling the loss situation. Some of the themes popular in current "realistic" fiction for children are death, divorce, moving, and adoption. *Books to Help Children Cope With Separation and Loss,* compiled by Joanne E. Bernstein (published by Bowker), is an excellent reference book available in many public libraries. Ms. Bernstein categorizes the books she lists according to the loss dealt with, and she describes each book in terms of the ages of children for whom it is intended, its main theme, its strengths, and its weaknesses. She also has an excellent introductory section that gives very helpful guidelines in using books to help children cope with separation and loss.

To be helpful, a book should present a realistic loss situation and offer believable characters. A child under six or seven may find it easier to identify with animals exhibiting human characteristics and feelings; by the age of seven or eight, the child will probably identify more readily with fictional children of his own age or slightly older.

If an adult chooses to use examples of people who have successfully coped with the same kind of loss, the child should be allowed to make his own comparisons and draw his own conclusions. If the child feels that he must meet a certain standard of coping, this imposes an extra burden on him and adds to his stress. One way of letting the child know that the offered example is not the only way of handling his loss, or even necessarily the "best" way, is to invite him to express his view of the book or person: "What do you think of the way Judy acted in this book? If you were Judy, do you think you would act the same way? In what ways do you think you might act differently from Judy?" These and similar questions can prompt a discussion of the example and help the child sort out what he chooses to imitate and what he wishes to reject. Conversations about an anecdotal or fictional example should be easy and informal, perhaps taking place little by little. The topic should be dropped when the child feels like abandoning it.

Offering Hope

A particular advantage in offering examples of others who have

131

coped with the same loss is the feeling of hope they can instill in the child. Grief often feels as if it has no beginning and will have no end; it may be difficult for the grieving child to imagine ever feeling any differently from the way he feels at this moment. Learning about others who have successfully negotiated the same tasks helps light a spark of hope in the darkness of the depression; it introduces the possibility, however faint at the time, that things may eventually change for the better.

Helplessness and a loss of control over his life are part of a child's feelings of grief. Discussing examples of others who have suffered loss offers the child the possibility that he might have some choices in his grief situation; he is not totally out of control. Choices may also be available in restructuring life after the loss. In the case of changing schools, the child may have a choice of walking or riding the bus; he may be able to choose between making his own lunch and having a hot lunch at school.

LOSING A SIGNIFICANT PERSON

The tasks of mourning for the child who has lost a significant person are essentially the ones I have described. The child may exhibit a period of intense identification with the person he has lost, in either a positive or a negative way. He may tend to idolize the person, seeing him as a superhuman embodiment of all virtue, wisdom, and strength, or he may find in him nothing good or worthy of respect or love. His behavior may be active rebellion against what the person stands for in his mind, or it may be a constant attempt to behave in a way pleasing to that person. Gradually there will be a lessening of his attachment to the person he has lost; he will internalize the qualities of that individual (or their opposites) and will compile a memory. In time the child will come to a point at which he can "let go" of the person he has lost, at the same time gaining a new perspective and a more complete picture of who he was—a more objective appraisal that includes both strengths and weaknesses. The child's emotional energy is gradually less involved with the person and more available for the activities and relationships that will make up his new "normal" life.

Recovery from grief, we recall, is not "forgetting" the person who has gone. Rather, it is the child's accepting the fact that this person is no longer an active part of his present or future life, while at the same time retaining the person as a part of his past and his memories. Sometimes the fear of forgetting an important person completely is part of a child's grief; he fears the recovery from grief, feeling that this recovery itself will take the individual away from him even more completely than the loss itself did. Grief is sometimes felt as the last link with the one he loved and lost, and he is afraid that recovery from grief will remove that final link. It is reassuring to the child to know that someone he loved remains with him; the person will always be a part of the child's past life, and he will generally retain a fairly vivid memory of him. In fact, as the feelings of grief soften, the memory of the one lost tends to become more present and real.

A child can be prepared for an anticipated loss of a loved one. Expected changes in the child's life can be discussed; if the loss comes through a move or divorce, rather than death, changes in the other person's life can also be talked about. Help in compiling a memory and establishing links with the person can be provided by pictures of the new home, a scrapbook of reminders, and an address and telephone number.

After the move, the divorce, or the death, it is helpful if there is an older child or an adult willing to talk about the child's loss. This may be a task for a friend of the family who knew the one lost, but who is less involved emotionally and can listen objectively to the child's memories.

The child's work of mourning in the loss of a special relationship varies greatly, depending on the age of the child, the nature of the loss, and the nature of the relationship. This kind of loss is the subject of the next chapter.

What Would Happen If . . ."

Some teaching of our children lies in the realm of "what to do if" or "what would happen if." We have fire drills, not because we expect to have a fire, but because the time when a fire breaks out is not the time to teach children how to exit from a building safely. We consider how to use the telephone in an emergency, fervently hoping and praying that the emergency will never happen. So, too, there are preparations that can be made with all children to prepare them for the death of parents or grandparents or other significant adults, not because these deaths are imminent, but because they can have a measure of knowledge, confidence, and security whenever they are eventually faced with these deaths.

Just as a child should know the exits and escape routes from his home, school, and church in the event of a fire, he should also know, I believe, what would happen to him in the event of the death of a parent or both parents during his childhood.

My own children know the general terms of my husband's will and my own. We have talked about "what would happen if daddy died," "what would happen if mommy died," and "what would happen if both mommy and daddy died." The important points for the children to know include where they would be likely to live, whether a move would be probable, whether the loss would entail a change of school or church, and possibly whether there would be a significant change in the family's financial status. It is also important for them to know whether mommy would go to work if daddy died; whether daddy would do the cooking and housework if mommy died; and most important, who will care for them (or at least the fact that there would be someone to take care of them). Most children are also interested in the question of remarriage: Would mommy or daddy marry again if the other one died?

As a personal life record, my husband and I also keep picture albums and card scrapbooks for each child, updating them about once a year. In the event of the loss of either or both of us, each child has ready access to some reminders for compiling a memory.

Preparing a child for the possible, but not imminently expected death of a parent during childhood should be relatively casual and low-key. The best way to do this is to answer his questions as they arise or give him information as it comes to mind: "By the way, daddy and I are thinking about buying a lot in the cemetery near the church" or "Grandma and grandpa said that they would like to be buried back near their old home" or "Aunt Jan said she would be happy to have daddy and me put her in our will as your guardian, if anything happens to both of us and you need a guardian." These casual statements may spark a discussion with the child or seem to fall on deaf ears. If the parent is open to talking about the subject, the child will ask questions when he is ready for information. A child's questions should be answered honestly and briefly, allowing him to ask for as much information as he wants and trying not to give him more than he desires.

Children generally manage to negotiate the tasks of mourning adequately and fairly easily, even without a lot of outside help. The presence of caring, supportive adults in their lives—adults who will accept them, listen to them, and love them—is the greatest help they can have in times of grief. It is often all the help they need. The additional aids suggested in this chapter may make the work of mourning somewhat smoother and easier for a child; they will probably not lessen the feelings of grief or do away with the pain. The suggestions are only suggestions; they may apply in part to many children, but no one child will need or benefit from all of them. If the adult listens to the child, loves him, and accepts him, his own intuition and imagination will usually show him the most effective ways to help the child in his unique situation.

7 THE LOSS OF SPECIAL RELATIONSHIPS

THE DEEPEST LOSS WE CAN suffer as human beings is a relationship with someone we have loved deeply. The grief experienced in this kind of loss is devastating; the task of mourning is difficult and may seem unbearable. How can we ever find life "normal" again? How can we make the transition from life with the one we loved to life without him? A deep part of ourselves is torn away with the loss of someone we love. How can we feel and be whole again?

To experience this depth of grief and mourning, we must have achieved a certain level of emotional maturity. We must be able to give of ourselves in a relationship and to receive the gift of another. This requires a certain degree of self-knowledge, self-acceptance, and self-control; it requires also the willingness to risk being known, the ability to accept another, and commitment. All these qualities are learned; they develop gradually in a child as he grows emotionally, as his knowledge of himself increases, and as he learns to interact with others.

Not all relationships acquire the same depth and mutuality, even between mature, stable adults. We tend to have a variety of relationships, all having different importance and meaning to us, all of varying intensity and levels of involvement. Not all losses of relationships result in severe grief and difficult mourning; some are relatively minor losses and bring moderate grief and mourning.

To help a child with the task of mourning the loss of a relationship, we need to consider the nature of the relationship itself. In particular, we need an awareness of the child's emotional development in his ability to form relationships, as this will affect the meaning of the relationship to him and thus the meaning of its loss.

RELATIONSHIPS IN INFANCY

In the first year of life, relationship is limited to dependency. Up to nine months of age, an infant may not distinguish between himself and others. Therefore the loss of a significant person in the infant's life cannot properly be termed the loss of a relationship. His world is extremely restricted, and the significant people are probably limited to mother, father, and possibly siblings.

An infant can suffer the loss of a parent through adoption, illness, death, or divorce. However, as long as his physical needs are met and he receives love and acceptance, he will probably not experience any grief over the loss at this time.

The loss of a parent or parents in infancy may be recognized as a loss, resulting in grief and mourning, when the child reaches adolescence. This is illustrated by the adopted child who suddenly wants to know who his "real" parents are. This can occur in a loving, accepting home, where there is a warm, understanding relationship between the child and his adoptive parents. This may also occur for the child whose mother or father was lost to him in infancy through death or divorce, even when the remaining parent has remarried and there is a comfortable, loving relationship with the stepparent.

The adolescent's primary task is to develop an identity of his own and to achieve independence. When he is trying to find out who he is, family identity may become important. The adolescent must "make a break" with the parents and become a person in his own right; to do this successfully, he usually needs the parents' presence, either in actuality or in the form of a strong memory. It is usually harder to make a break with an absent parent than with one who has been present during his struggle for individuality.

The process of an adolescent's achieving personal identity and independence is a form of mourning for the parents. During the process, the adolescent "loses" his parents as he gives up his childhood relationship with them and proceeds to regain them in a new, more mature relationship. This involves strong identification with the parents; an internalization of parental values, views, and characteristics as these are integrated into the emerging individuality; and, finally, the freeing of emotions invested in the childhood relationship and reinvesting this emotional energy in the new relationship.

Amid these emotional and psychological tasks, the adolescent may discover for the first time the importance of the loss of a parent or parents in infancy. In his struggle for identity and independence, he may need to mourn the loss of the absent parent or parents to complete the work of adolescence.

The adults in an infant's life may wish to prepare for the possible future need of the child to know and mourn his parent. They may anticipate this future need of the child as they compile a memory of the person who has gone in their own work of mourning. They may put aside photographs of the absent parent, jot down anecdotes about him, and save some of his treasured possessions that have special meaning in defining him.

Emotional trauma to the infant as a result of the loss of a parent can be minimized if stability is maintained in his life and his physical and emotional needs continue to be met. An adult can help an infant best by coping successfully with his own grief and mourning. Threats to the infant's security usually arise from the grief and mourning of the significant adults in his life—the remaining parent, grandparents, and possibly other relatives or close friends. These threatening factors include disruption of household schedule and routine; decreased attention; and loss of the presence of other significant adults due to withdrawal and depression wrought by grief.

Because death, serious illness, or divorce in a family represents a major loss for the significant adults, it is probably impossible to prevent these from having some effect on the infant. The infant's losses, however, lie in the loss of affection, attention, and care.

THE TWO-TO-FOUR-YEAR-OLD

Most of the same considerations hold true for the two–to–four-year-old. The primary relationship of a child this age is with himself. He is largely preoccupied with his body and its functions and seeking mastery over it. The loss of relationship for this child impinges on his relationship with himself and his own growing knowledge and control of his own body. The most common example of this is the loss of the "blankey," which was discussed earlier. The "blankey" is an extension of the child, and its loss is a loss of relationship. Other forms of a loss of relationship would be those involving his body due to illness or injury.

Losing a significant person is not yet a relationship loss for the two-to-four-year-old. Its impact on the child lies in the loss of security, dependability of routine, and stability. The child's grief and mourning will generally result from these intangible losses rather than the loss of a personal relationship.

This child still has a relatively limited world. Like the infant, he is limited to a few significant people in his life—those who determine and affect the pattern of his daily life. Again, these are usually parents and siblings; relatives or close friends are significant to the degree they are involved in the child's daily or weekly routine.

Feeling Rejected

Of special importance to a two-to-four-year-old is the feeling of rejection he is likely to experience in the loss of a significant person. The child has a limited view of death, disease, or divorce. He still views "big people" as omnipotent. He can scarcely conceive of an adult as having no choice in or control over his departure; his security is still too dependent on adults for him to risk admitting to himself that they, too, are limited. The adults' ability to control and order things beyond the child's control is part of the stability of his universe. Therefore, if a significant adult is lost to him through illness, death, or divorce, the child believes that the adult chose to go. In the child's self-centered universe, the fact that the adult chose to go away and leave him is experienced as a personal rejection.

Feelings of rejection include hurt, anger, and guilt. The child may react to these feelings in various ways. Most of his behavior is unconsciously designed to bring back the adult who has gone and thereby erase his loss. The child may regress, returning in behavior to an earlier age when the adult was present and the child felt accepted and loved. The child may become "very good," trying to win the favor and therefore the return of the absent adult. On the other hand, he may "act out" in ways, positive or negative, that are guaranteed to get attention from the absent adult. The child's behavior will rarely be consistent but more likely a confusing combination of these responses.

Loss As "Punishment"

By the age of two or three a child already has a firm association of "good behavior" with rewards and "bad behavior" with punishment. Punishment is experienced as unpleasant and may bring feelings of rejection. The loss of a significant adult often produces feelings that the child associates with punishment; he feels "punished" in the loss of someone on whom he depends. This leads to the conclusion that he has been guilty of "bad behavior," which results in feeling guilty. The feeling of rejection reinforces the feeling of guilt, since rejection in the child's life has often been the result of something he did wrong. (No matter how hard we try, we cannot completely separate rejection of a child's behavior from rejection of him as a person; especially for the very young child, the way he behaves and who he is are too closely allied in his own feelings and perceptions of himself to allow us to communicate acceptance of the person when we obviously reject the behavior.)

Guilt feelings in the child of this age—and in fact in children of all ages—are probably best dealt with at face value. Explanations that "Mommy didn't die because you shouted at her" or "Daddy didn't go away because you were too noisy" are necessary and should be offered. However, these explanations may have little or no impact on the guilt feelings, since they reach the child on an intellectual level. Guilt feelings need to be dealt with on an emotional level; they require confession and forgiveness. The child may be encouraged to confess his "bad behavior" to an adult who represents authority and to accept that adult's assurance of forgiveness. He may also be encouraged to confess his "badness" to God in prayer and be reminded that God has promised to forgive His children who confess their sins and ask for forgiveness.

Simultaneous with the hurt and guilt, the child may feel outrage and anger toward the adult who has abandoned him. This anger may increase his guilt; he may feel instinctively that it is "wrong" to be angry with grandpa for dying or with mommy for being sick. He may find these guilt feelings reinforced by adults who tell him, directly and nonverbally, what he "should" be feeling: "Can't you see how sick mommy is? You should feel sorry for her and try to help her get well!" or "Uncle didn't want to go away either. You should feel sorry for him; he's probably lonely and missing his family too."

The feelings of anger, their recognition, and responses to them have already been discussed. It may be an important step for the adults involved with the angry child to realize the difference between feelings and actions, however. Feelings themselves are not "good" or "bad"; the action we take as a result of the feelings is what is "good" or "bad." If adults can accept and believe this concept, they will be able to help a child accept his own feelings while he simultaneously learns to control the behavior he permits himself to indulge in expressing those feelings.

THE CHILD OF FIVE AND OLDER

At about age five, a child begins to move into the world of interpersonal relationships. He has mastered his own body and its functions; he is ready to begin school, meet new people, make friends, and "fall in love" with his teacher. As he walks out the front door, literally and figuratively, his life becomes more and more a matter of relationships. His world becomes more populated, and the people become important to him in varying degrees. For this child, the loss of a person will entail some loss of relationship. Age-related emotional developments are somewhat less important here than the way in which the relationship was lost. The degree of mutuality and intensity of the relationship does affect the severity of the grief and mourning.

As the child develops an increasing number of relationships, there are obviously more people in his life whose loss would bring grief. A significant person for an infant means primarily a mother or mother-substitute; for the two-to-four-year-old, the rest of the family circle and some close friends are included; from age five and up, the number of significant people may grow to include teachers, classmates, neighbors, and church friends.

The child comes to see people increasingly as unique individuals. People become less and less interchangeable in his life. Thus he may find that the fourth-grade teacher, however delightful in her own right, does not really take the place of the third-grade teacher. When talking about grandparents, the child will find it necessary to clarify which grandpa or grandma is meant; the differences in personality outweigh the identity of blood relationship.

The loss of a parent remains one of the most significant losses a person can experience throughout childhood, adolescence, and adulthood. Initially the parents' world completely surrounds the child's world. As the child grows older, goes to school, and makes his own friends, he develops a portion of his world that is not shared by the parents. However, the portion not shared by the parents is relatively small, at least until adolescence. Therefore, the loss of a parent includes an enormous number of intangible losses. Almost no part of the child's life is left unchanged by this loss; few things can "go on as usual" after he loses a parent. The mother is often more completely involved and more continually present in the child's life than the father is; thus the loss of the mother can be more encompassing than the loss of the father.

Assuming the Role

Mourning the loss of a parent follows basically the tasks of mourning described in chapter 3, except in its magnitude and the great number of intangible losses. There is potentially, however, one significant distinction. During the period of identification with the lost parent, the child may feel that he must take over that person's role and responsibilities. Susie may feel that she must be the "woman of the house, now that mommy has died"; Johnny may believe he is "the man of the house" after his father's departure.

Carl Smith was eight when his father died in his early forties. Bob had been an active, athletic outdoorsman. He had spent much time playing baseball and basketball, hiking, boating, and fishing with his children. Eight months before his death, he developed stomach pains. When they grew too painful to ignore and were interfering with his routine and work, he finally went to the doctor. He was found to have an advanced case of cancer of the pancreas. Surgery would avail little; there was a slim chance that chemotherapy might help. However, Bob was not one of the few who respond to treatment in this disease. There came a day in the hospital when Bob and his wife realized he had only a short time to live.

Bob decided to go home. He wanted to be with his family as much as possible and to spend his last days in his own home with them. To this point, Carl and four-year-old Joanna had known that daddy was sick, but they were expecting him to get well. Margery Smith confronted me that day in the hospital with tears streaming down her face: "What do we tell the children? How can we tell them what's happening?" I didn't answer, but looked at Bob. Bob grasped his wife's hands and said, "Honey, leave this to me. I'll tell them. I can do that much for you—and for them."

"But they'll cry, and I'll cry. I don't want the kids to see me cry!"

Bob held Margery and looked at me. I told her, "It's natural that you'll cry. You don't want your children to think that you don't care about Bob, do you? When you are losing someone you love, of course you cry! It's natural, normal, and very much all right. Your tears will upset the children less than if you don't cry, for they would wonder whether you really care about Bob at all."

The next time I saw the Smith family was after the funeral. Everyone seemed to be handling the situation well. We sat in the Smiths' family room, drank coffee, and talked about the funeral. Carl stayed close to his mother, and Joanna climbed into my lap.

I was a little surprised to get a phone call from Margery a week or two later, asking if we could get together and talk. She was concerned about Carl. There was nothing really specific: He was eating and sleeping normally, and his grades in school were good; but he spent little time away from Margery. He continued to play with his friends, but he usually brought them into the house, within view and earshot of his mother, instead of going outside or to their homes. His manners were almost too good, and he almost never argued or fought with his sister.

We were fortunate in knowing a therapist who was experienced in using children's drawings to interpret emotional states. Carl and Joanna were both asked to draw a picture. They chose a large box of colorful crayons and a stack of paper. Joanna's drawing was a landscape with green grass, brilliant flowers, and a small house. The colors were bright and alive; the only thing missing was the sun. "It's there," she explained to us, "only it's behind the clouds right now, and you can't see it."

Carl's picture was very different. It was a large, angry sea done in the darkest shade of blue he could find. The strokes were bold and sharp. Dominating the entire scene was a huge black shark. The shark's open mouth was filled with rows and rows of terrifying sharp teeth. Carl took a lot of time and trouble to draw those teeth. There were no bright colors in the picture in spite of the wide selection of crayons available; it was somber and a bit menacing.

Donna, the therapist, took Carl on a short walk and talked with him about the picture. "Carl, that's quite a scary shark you drew. It sure has a lot of big, sharp teeth. Are you trying to say that you feel that things are scary right now?"

Carl put his hand in Donna's and looked up at her. "I'm too little to be the man of the family!" he blurted. "I don't know how to do it!"

Well-meaning friends and relatives had come to Carl after his father's death and told him, "You need to take care of your mother and sister now. You're the man of the family!" Carl was old enough to have some idea of what this meant. He was still a little boy; he didn't feel that he was old enough or big enough to take his father's place. The burden of responsibility and the insecurity of not knowing how to handle it had been the problem his mother and relatives couldn't quite identify. Carl and Donna, and later Carl and his mother, had several long talks. He was reassured that it was all right for him to be a little boy; he didn't have to grow up all at once and be the man of the family. He could still depend on his mother, as a boy needs to, and he didn't need to be responsible for her.

Later on, Donna asked Carl to draw a picture of his family. In this picture the family was taking a boat trip. The water was vivid with blues and greens. A sun shone from the upper righthand corner. The entire boat and even the motor were done in gold. At one end of the boat was a stick figure, child-size, representing Joanna. Sitting in the boat was Bob, his stick-figure the smallest in the drawing. Behind the wheel of the boat, steering, was Carl; close behind Carl, with her hands on his shoulders, was his mother. Carl was still representing himself as the "man of the family," but with an enormous difference! Mother was there behind him—holding him, helping him, guiding him. With the feeling of being able to depend on mother and her comfort, the "darkness" over Carl lifted, symbolized in the bright, lively colors of his second picture.

A Fine Line

When a man loses his wife, or a woman her husband, it is natural to turn to the children for comfort. This is normal, expected, and good. The child himself may be comforted and helped in his grief by finding that he has something of value to offer his remaining parent.

However, there is a fine line between allowing a child, as himself, to be a comfort and companion to us in our loss and asking

145

him to erase the loss by taking the person's place, by "becoming" that person. To ask the child to become "the man of the house" or "the little mother" places an unwarranted, unfair burden on the child. This is more a matter of attitude than of actual chores and duties. A girl of eleven or twelve (or even eight or nine) may take over many of the household tasks that her mother used to perform and remain her "little girl" self instead of becoming "the woman of the house," or "the little mother." If she has the security of being allowed to remain a little girl—to act, think, and feel like one, to ask for help and advice from her father and other relatives—the added tasks will not be an overwhelming burden. Carl's second picture symbolizes this beautifully: He was willing to take the wheel of the boat—figuratively speaking—as long as his mother was behind him, offering him her love and support.

During the period of intense identification, it is easy for a child to slip into the absent parent's role. The adults whom the child loves and trusts can help to prevent him from feeling the burden of having to adopt and keep that role, however. By affirming him for who he is (not simply for being "just like your dad") and by allowing him to express feelings of uncertainty, insecurity, and dependence (instead of telling him, "You can't cry; you have to be the man of the family now"), adults open the way for the child to move into the next phase of mourning. This phase involves sorting through the ways he wishes to be like his father and the ways he does not want to be like him. The child may then genuinely integrate parts of his absent father into his own personality and abandon the somewhat artificial likeness that is part of the earlier intense identification.

As in other loss situations, negative identification with a lost parent is often more intense and more difficult to deal with than positive identification. This is not uncommon in the child who feels an intense anger for the parent who is gone; it is probably more common in the case of divorce than in illness or death. A response to this child that approaches his feelings is more likely to be helpful than one that focuses on his behavior.

Loss of a Sibling

There is another loss situation in which a child may feel compelled to "become" the lost member of the family. In the loss of a child who has siblings, the remaining child or children may feel a need to "make up" the loss to the parents. Although a child may come to this decision on his own, in most cases he is encouraged to this choice by the parents themselves or by other significant adults. If the child perceives that his parents had high expectations of the lost child and are devastated by the loss, he may attempt to take the absent child's place. This may be true especially if the absent child has run away or broken the relationship completely somehow. The parents may express extreme disappointment and hurt—"Helen was always the bright one in the family, and now she'll never get to go to college, since she ran away and got married like that"—so Helen's sister Sue may feel obligated to go to college and take her place.

Again, the most effective way of dealing with this over-identification with the absent sibling is to affirm the child in his uniqueness. Comparisons between the remaining and absent siblings are probably harmful. The remaining one should be helped to feel that he has a special, irreplaceable position in the family. The information that "No one can ever take Helen's place" can be a comfort to Sue if it is expressed in such a way that she realizes it also holds true for her: No one can ever take her place either. Sue's identification with Helen after Helen's leaving should be tolerated if it comes, but neither encouraged nor discouraged. When Sue is ready to move away from the identification, she is less likely to feel guilty or defensive.

With relationships, the nature of the loss has a significant effect on the course and duration of mourning. Two of the most important variables in a loss are its permanence and its completeness. Losses that are definite and final and perceived as such by the child are more easily mourned than those that are indefinite or believed to be temporary. A complete loss may also be easier to handle than an alteration in the relationship, in which important parts are lost, but other important parts remain.

Permanent Vs. Temporary

The distinction between permanent and temporary losses becomes important only after the age at which the child has developed some understanding of time and the concept of the future. A child under two will experience all losses as permanent. From two to five, a child has learned to expect people who leave to come back, and he is likely to regard the loss as temporary; much of his work of mourning involves discovering permanence and the fact that to-day's loss extends into tomorrow. For a child past five, the distinction between temporary and permanent losses will influence the progress of the work of mourning.

When a loss is perceived by the child as temporary, the focus of the work of mourning is testing its reality and its permanence. This is particularly true in the loss of a parent through divorce. Such a loss is perceived, not only as temporary, but often as less than total. Testing the reality and permanence of the loss leads to trying to discover its extent. Due to the change of the relationship between the parents, the child's relationship with the divorced parent is altered—but not totally lost. Therefore, much of the child's work of mourning is exploring this alteration in relationship and its meaning for his own daily, weekly, and monthly routine.

Loss Through Divorce

Loss through death may be easier for the child in some respects than loss through divorce. Ceremony and ritual surround death; there is a sense of finality and termination. In divorce, there is no formal ritual or ceremony marking the loss for the child. Moreover, the adults whom the child loves and trusts may hinder his testing of the loss and its extent by acting as if nothing has changed. Divorce is not quite as final as death, especially to the child. A child's natural tendency to deny the loss is strengthened by the possibility—if only in the child's mind—of a reconciliation between the parents. (If either parent clings to the hope of reconciliation, or grandparents or other important adults hold onto this hope, the child's mourning may be even more difficult.) Initially this child may react to his loss in the same way as a child who moves away from home temporarily, with the expectation of returning. The child may also react with a strong identification with the absent parent and show a remarkable persistence in attempting to reconcile his divorced parents.

Exploring the alteration in relationship and its meaning in the child's life may be difficult. The divorced parent who has left may reappear in a random and unpredictable fashion. The change of his place in the child's life and his position in relationship may be vague and ill-defined. The child may go for weeks without seeing daddy or even talking to him on the phone, only to wake up one Saturday morning and find that all his own plans for the day have to be canceled because daddy is coming to take him out.

Divorce is probably more difficult to discuss with a child than death is. As hard as it is to talk about anticipated changes because of the death of a parent, it is even more difficult to talk about changes resulting from divorce. To "spare" the child from facts such as custodial arrangements, visiting privileges, plans for summer vacations and other holidays, and some financial arrangements increases insecurity and uncertainty. Instead of "sparing" the child, it may actually make his grief and mourning more difficult and protracted. In divorce—where the child suffers a permanent, but partial loss of an important relationship—adults can help him discover the extent of his loss. Some confusion and uncertainty can be eliminated if the basic aspects of the divorce settlement as they relate to him are shared with him: "You are going to live with mommy. Daddy will come and see you every Thursday night, and he will take you home with him every other weekend." This clear, precise, factual information is more helpful than telling the child, "Daddy isn't gone forever. He's still your daddy. You'll still get to see him."

Other Situations

There are other situations in which a child's loss is perceived as temporary or is restricted to certain aspects of a relationship. One is the birth of a sibling. The child experiences loss in a change of relationship with his parents. The focus of this work of mourning (usually brief and not generally difficult) lies in discovering the extent of the loss in daily routine, time and attention from mommy and daddy, and exclusive right to toys or room or other things that must be shared with the new baby. The birth of a sibling often occurs when a child is between the ages two and five; for him, discovering the extent of his loss also requires learning about its permanence. It is not uncommon for a three-or-four-year-old to ask, "When are we going to take the new baby back to the hospital?" implying, "When is life going to return to normal?"

The serious illness of a significant person also results in the loss of relationship. This may be partial and temporary, or it may progress into a terminal illness and the permanent, complete loss inherent in death. A serious illness of one important person generally involves loss of relationship with others as well; others may become less available to the child, for example. The illness of a sibling involves a loss of time and attention from both parents as well as the sibling's companionship. Mother's illness means that father is busier and more preoccupied and therefore has less time for the child; grandma's or grandpa's illness may take mother or father away from home for a period of days or weeks and temporarily affect the parent's relationship with the child.

If the illness is short-term, there is probably no need to take special measures to help the child in his grief and mourning. However, a serious illness lasting more than several weeks introduces a variety of intangible losses that need to be identified and mourned. Perhaps the most important aspect of the child's grief will be his loss of security and stability. Setting new schedules, routines, and family patterns that can be adhered to for the duration of the illness will introduce a measure of order and security into the child's life. If these changes can be discussed with the child, and if he can participate in the decision-making, he gains a measure of control over the situation which will reduce his sense of helplessness and frustration.

SUDDEN LOSS VS. ANTICIPATED LOSS

Another factor that influences the child's grief and mourning is the way he experiences the loss. If it is sudden and unexpected, the child's grief and work of mourning all take place after the loss has occurred. If the loss follows a long illness and is anticipated, the child is able to begin his work of mourning before it becomes final. Even if the child is "protected" from the knowledge that grandma's illness is likely to result in death, he may pick up enough nonverbal information to begin the work of mourning before grandma dies.

In cases where the death of a loved one is the result of a disease process, the child can be helped by explanations of the disease, how it progresses, and why it causes death. Explanations are particularly important to a child of nine or older. These explanations should be simply stated and cover only as much information as the child desires. Reasons for the death are probably more important in the case of a sudden death than with a progressive illness and an anticipated death; in sudden death, the one who died may have appeared perfectly well and healthy only days or hours before, and it is difficult to accept. With progressive illness, physical changes are often observable to the child.

An anticipated death may be easier to deal with than a sudden death. This is most likely to be the case if adults prepare the child for the loss by death. If there is a loved one at high risk for sudden death—as from a heart attack or a stroke—the child might also be prepared. The child can be informed casually of the risk and possibility of sudden death in the same way he can be informed of his parents' wills and arrangements made for him if he is orphaned. This information lies in the realm of "what to do if" or "what will happen if" teaching. The teaching can be done in a nonalarming manner—as a sharing of information, not as a sharing of deep concern or worry.

Accidental Death

Accidental death may be more difficult for a child to deal with than death by disease, whether sudden or anticipated. Accidents, because they are accidents, seem pointless and meaningless. The fact that they come "out of the blue" is unsettling and threatening to the security of the child's world. Anger is likely to be one of the strongest grief feelings in a loss by accidental death. The child's mourning work may focus largely on this anger and his dealing with it.

There is a strong tendency to look for someone to blame for an accidental death: The driver of the other car, the storekeeper who sold a ladder that slipped, the person who took Robert out in his boat, or even the person who died (for not preventing or avoiding the accident). Even after anger has been dealt with in the ways we have already suggested, it is necessary that the child face his blame of the one who "caused" the accident. The child has two choices: He may choose to forgive this person, or he may choose to live with an attitude of bitterness, resentment, and unforgiveness toward him.

The Need to Forgive

As with guilt, the issue of blame must be handled on two levels. The accuracy and fairness of the blame can be examined intellectually with the child. He may come to see that his blame was partly or completely unjustified; on the other hand, he may become further convinced of the guilt of the person he is blaming.

The second level involves dealing with the feelings of anger, bitterness, and unforgiveness that the child holds toward the person he blames. On this emotional level, the fairness or unfairness of the blame may have little impact. To resolve his bitterness and anger, the child needs to come to a point of forgiving the other person, whether the guilt is real or imagined.

To choose to forgive is seldom easy. It is least difficult in cases where the harm was unwitting and unintentional. But to refuse to forgive can burden the child with greater bitterness, corroding his spirit and creating inner tension. It can lead to a variety of physical symptoms and illnesses if allowed to continue.

Our first step in helping a child to forgive the one he blames for a death is to exhibit a forgiving attitude ourselves. If we cling to our own bitterness and unforgiveness, it is difficult to persuade a child to give up his. The next step is to help the child realize and admit that he is blaming someone for his loss. After that, the child needs to see that he has a choice between forgiving and not forgiving. He should be reminded that God teaches us to forgive those who have injured us, as He Himself forgives us. He may also need the reminder that God can help us to forgive, even when we are powerless to do so ourselves.

If the child has chosen to forgive, has asked for God's help, and still seems unable to rid himself of his bitter feelings, we may need to take additional steps. One way of coming to a point of forgiveness is to pray for the one who has wronged us. Another help is to replace thoughts of bitterness and revenge with other thoughts, especially thoughts of praise and thanks to God. Finally, the passage of time itself will be helpful. If the child has made the choice to forgive and has asked God's help in forgiving, we can feel free to assure the child that the bitter thoughts will go away and he will be able to feel forgiving eventually.

Loss by Suicide

The last instance of loss by death that deserves special consideration is suicide. One of the first questions a child or an adult asks about a suicide is "Why?" The first and simplest explanation for suicide is that the person was supremely unhappy. This was not ordinary unhappiness, but the extreme unhappiness of depression, which is a form of sickness.

Beyond that, the child is likely to react out of hurt and anger and look for someone to blame. He may also simultaneously feel guilty himself. If the suicide is a parent or other significant adult or a sibling, the child's feelings of rejection will be deep and long-lasting. The suicide of a parent also affects a child's self-esteem and identity severely.

Feelings of grief and the work of mourning in the case of a suicide tend to be severe and prolonged. Even with all our love, acceptance, and concern we may not be able to give this child adequate help; I believe that most children who lose a significant person by suicide should at least be offered the opportunity to receive counseling from a pastor, psychologist, or social worker.

Losing the Disliked

So far we have talked about grief and mourning as following the loss of something or someone loved. The truth is that grief and mourning can also result from the loss of something or someone we can't stand. Grief and mourning result from the loss of anything in which we have an emotional investment, whether positive or negative. A negative emotional attachment is frequently stronger than a positive one; its loss will undoubtedly occasion grief and mourning, perhaps more severe and difficult than the loss of something or someone deeply loved. In general, the work of mourning is the same whether the emotional involvement is positive or negative. In mourning someone he hated or strongly disliked, a child may discover attractive characteristics of the person. He may then regret the nature of his relationship with the lost person; he may also have to mourn the friendship he now sees as a lost opportunity.

CONCLUSION

Most children are able to negotiate the tasks of mourning in a healthy manner and emerge from their grief as stronger, growing people. The help of loving, accepting, sensitive adults provides a child with an even better chance of making a complete recovery from grief.

Because of all the variables in the nature of the relationship, the age of the child, and the way in which the relationship was lost, it is impossible to predict a timetable for completing the work of mourning. If there is evidence that the child is moving through the process of mourning and that his grief is lessening, there is usually no need for special concern or professional counseling. Children who need this kind of extra help are those whose work of mourning seems to be stalled or sidetracked. If the child shows no evidence of a gradual return to normal living and a gradual reawakening of old interests and involvement in new ones; if the child's eating is so disturbed that he gains or loses a significant amount of weight; if the child's sleeping patterns do not begin to return toward normal—in these cases there is cause for concern, and it might be wise to consult a counselor.

Other signs of possible distortion of mourning are the development of new, irrational fears; regression persisting for weeks or even months; a complete change of lifestyle without any signs of returning toward the former pattern even after weeks or months; or unnatural "best behavior" continuing for weeks and months after the loss. The child most likely to need help with his mourning work is the one who has suffered a number of serious losses in quick succession without an opportunity to mourn them completely; a child whose loss includes a large number of intangible losses—such as the death or divorce of a parent, move from the family home, change of schools, and loss of a pet—all within several months; children who have very ambivalent feelings about the lost person, particularly if it is a parent; and children who suffer a loss through suicide.

Consulting a counselor in no way indicates inadequacy or failure on the part of either the parent or the child. It is the wise person who knows when to ask for help and how to accept help when it is needed.

8 RECOVERING FROM GRIEF

AT THE POINT OF RECOVERING from grief, we are newborn. Some of our old life has been stripped from us—its habits, patterns, attachments, involvements. We have successfully negotiated the separation from that which we loved that was part of our life. We have found a place for it in our memories, and it is now a part of our past. It remains with us, yet the energy of emotional involvement is now free to find new directions and new attachments. There is a sense of relief, of cleansing, the lifting of the cloud of darkness that surrounded our grief, and the freedom from responsibilities and limitations that were necessarily, and perhaps joyfully, a part of what we have lost. Now, in a small or a large way, we can start over.

This approach to loss and grief is learned. It is never easy to lose something we care about, or even something that we take for granted as a part of our lives. The restructuring of life without that which was lost is often difficult and painful. Yet it has its rewards. After the Good Friday of our grief and mourning comes Easter Sunday, the day of resurrection and renewal.

To come to this point in grief and mourning requires something of us. To be able to help a child arrive at this place—to refrain from interfering as he picks his way cautiously and painfully through the grief of many "little deaths"—may be even more difficult. Still, the central message of the New Testament is one of death and resurrection. Life comes out of death; the part of a person that dies in each "little death" can be reborn in new and better ways.

There are many helps in the Christian faith for negotiating the transition periods between the death and the resurrection. The gos-

155

pel message has never been a denial of reality. God has not promised to make everything easy and painless, but He has promised redemption—redemption of our souls, but also of our bodies, our daily living, and ultimately all of Creation.

CHOOSING THE COURSE

In each loss situation, in each period of grief and mourning, we and our children are faced with choices. Although the circumstances of our lives are ordered for us, our responses and reactions are of our own choosing. No matter how strongly we are inclined toward one habit pattern, no matter how deep our conditioned reflexes and automatic responses, these are all open to change. And the change comes gradually or quickly as a result of our choices.

Our strongest influence on our children lies in who we are. Our attitudes and behavior speak to them far more meaningfully than our words. What we wish to see in them, we must be willing to work at in ourselves, in order to set an example and to mark the path for them. Thankfully, it is not necessary that we be perfect; if we are open to change and personal growth, this cannot help but have an effect on our children.

Denying our feelings of grief is not the answer. We cannot effectively deal with something we refuse to acknowledge. As we learn to accept our own feelings—sadness, anger, guilt, despair —we become better able to choose the ways we will deal with them. As we dare to allow our children to see our feelings and our own acceptance of these feelings, we free them to learn to accept and admit their feelings.

Feelings and actions, although closely connected, are distinct and separately determined. I do not believe that there are any "wrong" feelings; however, admitting and accepting them is not equivalent to license. We can accept feelings and yet set limits on what we will tolerate in ourselves and in our children regarding behavior. We can acknowledge and accept our feelings without letting them control us or dictate our actions. As we learn this for ourselves, we can help our children learn this as well.

The knowledge that we need not fear our feelings or what they will "make" us do because we have control and choice in our actions is a very liberating and comforting concept. Children fear some of their feelings, especially anger, because they are afraid the emotions will govern them and their responses will get out of control. Besides exhibiting for our children the fact that feelings do not need to govern our actions, we can help them by providing necessary limits and controls on their behavior until they are able to control their behavior themselves. Moreover, we can help them explore their options for expressing feelings and thus help them find acceptable and satisfying ways of dealing with their emotions.

Just as our feelings influence our behavior, so too our behavior affects our feelings. Our choice of behavior can influence the way we feel; if we act in a loving way and wish to become loving, we eventually feel loving. In addition, we tend to become what we think. The thoughts that we invite into our minds, cultivate, and make welcome eventually shape both behavior and feelings. Although we cannot control all our random thoughts, we can excercise some control over those thoughts we choose to allow to remain and become habits of mind.

THE HABIT OF PRAISE

One habit of mind that is repeatedly commanded us in Scripture is praise. God deserves our praise; He is worthy of it; and He demands it. The choice to praise God in thought and word is ours to make. It does not matter whether we "feel like" praising God; the act of praising Him, in obedience to His Word, will eventually produce in us the habit and feelings of praise. Praise of God is a marvelous antidote to depression and can lighten the load of grief. Praising Him lifts the mind, heart, and soul into the presence of God and opens us to His healing love. Praise of God is something we can teach our children, by direct instruction and by example. We can order our daily schedule as families so that we begin and end the day in praise of God; this may be by use of the Psalms, the words of the Epistles, the hymns of the church, the words of Christian writers, or our own words.

Closely allied to the habit of praise of God is the habit of thanking God. Praise of God differs from thanksgiving primarily in focus: In praise, we focus on God Himself; in thanksgiving we focus on His gifts to us. Thanksgiving to God is another habit of mind to which the Scriptures exhort us. Like praise, the habit of thanksgiving can be cultivated. We can learn to turn each experience of joy and delight into an act of thanks to God. The birdsong in the early morning, the sunrise, the cooling rain, the spring flower can all offer occasions of joy that we learn to express in thanksgiving to God. It is just as easy to say, "Thank God for this beautiful day!" as to say, "Isn't it a glorious day?" As we learn to turn consciously to God in thanksgiving for the joy and beauty in our lives, we teach our children the same habit.

When grief unsettles us, rearranges our schedules and plans, throws the future into uncertainty, and leaves us feeling confused and bewildered, the habits of our daily living can be a source of stability and security. If we have incorporated praise and thanksgiving into our daily routine and family structure, this pattern not only provides stability, but also helps keep us open to the presence and love of God amid our grief. Each family can develop a ritual that is meaningful and makes praise and thanksgiving part of the daily pattern of living. There are also readymade rituals of praise and thanksgiving, especially in some of the more formal churches, which can be adapted by the family for its particular needs.

In my family there are several daily rituals that make the presence of God clear to us and help us develop and maintain habits of praise and thanksgiving. A common "Good morning" in our home is the phrase, "God loves you, and I do too," accompanied by a hug and a kiss. As the family members leave the breakfast table to go separate ways, we use a ritual farewell: "Go with God," and the response, "God be with you."

We have a prayer ritual, developed when the children were very young, which we call "Dear God, we are thankful." At these times we go around the family circle, each member in turn mentioning something for which he or she is thankful. As each item is mentioned, the family responds, "Dear God, we are thankful." We continue around the circle time after time, expressing our thanks to God for sunshine, rain, home and family, friends, flowers, toys, a good day in school, success in an undertaking, good books, fires in the fireplace—the list is inexhaustible, and we often have difficulty stopping. From time to time the children and I memorize and repeat Psalms together, on the way to school, on walks, or on shopping trips. Some of our favorites are Psalms 103, 100, 27, 34, 1, and 23. We also have hymnsings occasionally as an evening family activity.

In times of darkness and uncertainty, the memory of God's work in the past is a source of encouragement and motivation. We can remind ourselves and our children of the history of God's intervention in the lives of His people. This may be done by repeating familiar Bible stories or by reading of His work in the lives of other Christians, both our contemporaries and those who have gone before us. One very effective reminder of God's working is a family "salvation history"—a record of critical times in the life of the family, and the way in which God intervened. Another possibility is a prayer diary, recording the date of a prayer, what was prayed, and how and when God answered.

FEELING GOD'S LOVE

It is one thing to "know" and believe in God's love and goodness; it is another thing to feel it. The habits of praise and thanksgiving open us to receive God's love and grace; a review of His working in our lives and others' strengthens our trust and belief. However, it is valid and good to ask God to come to us and to our children in ways we can feel. For a young child in particular, feeling God's love is as important as knowing about it, and many times it is more important.

One way we can feel God's love is in the community of His people. The church is the body of Christ—His hands, His arms, His lap. In our times of grief we need the company of others, especially those of like mind and like faith. As we learn to turn to the community of believers for support and the tangible evidences of God's love, we teach our children to do the same.

As parents we represent God to our children in a unique way. We are the closest members of the body of Christ to them. Sometimes we need to say to our children, "I know you can't feel that God loves you right now; but you can feel and know that I love you. Right now, God's love for you is the love you can feel from me." This may later be expanded to include the love the child feels from others who, as members of Christ's body on earth, are His physical, visible representatives.

In each of us there is the person God created—the person one is meant to be. God's purpose in our lives is to make us who we truly are. Salvation and redemption mean the complete restoration in each of us of the image of God.

Remember the story of Eustace in chapter 3? God is Aslan, tearing the dragon skin so that the person may emerge, naked and hurting, to be clothed in new clothes and seated as a guest at the wedding banquet. He is the Sculptor, using a variety of tools to chip away the overlying marble that obscures the design He sees in us. Growing spiritually, seen in this light, is not so much a matter of learning new things or acquiring new skills as a shedding of the concealing skins, a stripping down to the essential "real" person God made us to be.

The culmination of this process lies in the future. This is the promise and the hope of the Resurrection. Until that time, we must be incomplete and unfinished. At that time, "we shall be like him, for we shall see him as he is" (1 John 3:2). This likeness encompasses our total being—body, emotions, mind, spirit. Rather than warring against one another, or limiting and inhibiting one another, the various aspects of ourselves will know union and integration.

The hope of the Resurrection—bodily, physical, future—is the great hope of our faith, stressed again and again by the New Testament writers. Not only will our spirits, emotions, and minds be reborn and "resurrected" as we survive the "little deaths" of our lives, but our bodies also are promised resurrection and redemption.

Since the concept of resurrection is so central to Christian teaching, we need to impart it to our children. The scriptural image of the resurrection body uses the analogy of a seed and the plant which grows from it; our present body and our resurrection body are respectively the seed and the plant.

Although I am not an expert gardener, I am able to recognize a variety of different seeds by their size, shape, color, and other characteristics. I am able to recognize the relationship of the tomato seed to the tomato plant, the pepper seed to the shiny green pepper leaves, the round and dark radish seeds to their firm red globes, and the tiny and fragile lettuce seeds to the lacy green leaves of the lettuce.

In the seed-plant analogy, God has given us—as He so often does—a visible, physical aid to understanding a deep spiritual truth. The analogy is one children can grasp and understand.

Since we are not given much information regarding the exact

nature of the resurrection body (probably because we are not capable of comprehending its exact definition), we must rely on symbols and analogies in teaching the meaning of the resurrection to our children. Yet, even without precise definition there is a sense of excitement surrounding the teaching of the resurrection. Whatever it is that is in store for us, it is greater and better than that which we have now! The plant with its leaves, flowers, and fruit is so very much more than the seed.

The other scriptural analogy describing the resurrection body is clothing. When we have become truly ourselves, stripped of the "skins" and coverings that hide us from ourselves and others as the person God created, we are ready for "new clothes" (2 Cor. 5). Physical death, in view of the hope of the resurrection, can be compared to exchanging a set of drab, worn-out, imperfectly fitting clothes for new garments that fit perfectly and complement, reveal, and enhance all that we are.

Ultimately the integration of our faith into our teaching of our children about loss, grief, and mourning lies in the communication of hope. It is the Christian hope that God is working in our lives; hope that the image of God and a likeness to Christ will emerge in us; hope for emotional maturity and integration; and the hope of being fitted—body, soul, and spirit—for the redeemed creation God has promised.

APPENDIX 1
THE THEOLOGY OF DEATH

DEATH HAS A CENTRAL place in Christian theology. The definition and meaning of life and the nature and purpose of man are intricately bound up in our understanding of death.

The first mention of death in the Bible comes in the Creation account in Genesis. Before the creation of man, God spoke the word, and the world and all that is in it sprang into being. The creation of man was different: God Himself formed a physical body for man, then He Himself breathed into this body a living soul. So from the beginning man was different from the rest of creation; he was made by a special act of God, and his life derived from God in a special way. He received a physical body and a living soul; he was made in the image of God.

There is no mention of death until after the Creation. After making man, male and female, in His image, God provided a garden home and gave them authority and responsibility for the rest of His world. He gave the man and woman all the fruit of the garden for their food with one exception. Genesis 2:17 says, "You must not eat from the tree of the knowledge of good and evil, for when you eat of it you will surely die." The King James Version renders the word *when* as "in the day." There was a divine prohibition, and the result of disobedience to it was to be death.

At that point Adam and Eve did not know the meaning of death. They learned death by disobedience. The record states that they disobeyed by eating the forbidden fruit. They did *not* experience physical death that very day. Perhaps the King James phrase "In the day that thou eatest thereof" is not of great significance—but what actually happened in the day when they ate the fruit?

The serpent, tempting Eve to disobey God, said, "No, you would not die at all!" (Gen. 3:4, *Modern Language Bible*). If physical death were all that God had meant by His statement, "You will surely die," then the serpent was more accurate than the Almighty. Suppose God did indeed mean "that very day" and the serpent's reassurances were merely a clever half-truth: What does this tell us about death?

In the day of disobedience, separation was introduced into the world. Until that time, there was harmony and unity: Adam with Eve, Adam and Eve with all of creation, the created world with God. After the disobedience came a division in creation: The separation of Adam and Eve from each other, creation, and God.

The first evidence of this separation is that Adam and Eve made aprons for themselves, hiding their bodies from each other.

Next comes evidence of separation from God. We have the picture, before the disobedience, of God walking with Adam and Eve in the garden in the cool of the evening. Now, when they hear the voice of God walking in the garden, they hide. God calls them, and they answer that they are afraid.

When they meet God and are faced with their disobedience, they again display the separation that has occurred between them. It is a matter of "each one for himself." Adam blames Eve, and Eve blames the serpent. In answering God's questions, they move apart from each other so as not to be responsible for the other's actions.

God then announces the further results of their disobedience: The ground would be cursed because of this human act. Instead of harmony between man and creation, man would have to fight with the ground to force it to yield its fruits. Labor would be mixed with sorrow, fruit with thorns and thistles, health and growth with sickness and decay (see Gen. 3).

Finally, the separation and alienation introduced into creation would be known in man's very self. The man and his wife had already experienced a sense of shame toward their bodies. Now God told the woman that the natural processes of life would find pain and sorrow mixed with their joy. Reproduction, begun in the intimacy and ecstasy of sexual union, would end with labor and travail; the joy of new life would be preceded by the sorrow and pain of childbirth.

The culmination of this discord is expressed spiritually in Paul's cry in the New Testament: "I know that nothing good lives in me, that is, in my sinful nature. For I have the desire to do what is good, but I cannot carry it out. For what I do is not the good I want to do; no, the evil I do not want to do—this I keep on doing" (Rom. 7:18–19). Materially the culmination is the final separation of physical death, in which the body is separated from the soul and spirit; man, who was created a living soul within a physical body, experiences the tearing apart of body and soul.

One evidence of the extent of this separation is the easy way we dichotomize ourselves into body and spirit, with the accompanying condemnation of one half. Most of us live a life in which we psychologically and spiritually separate the spirit-soul from the body. For Christians, there is a tendency to reject our physical aspects and affirm what we consider "spiritual." Yet it was not the body that sinned; it merely gave expression to the will of man.

A BALANCED VIEW

A balanced view of the meaning of death and a balanced view of the nature of man go hand-in-hand. We are body; we were created as body. I know myself as a body: The image I see in the mirror, the muscles that tire with exercise, the sound of my voice, the shape of my hands, even the characteristic pattern of my footsteps as I walk or run. This is I!

Similarly, we know each other as physical beings. We describe and define each other by means of the physical world. I know my family and friends by their voices and faces, by the feel of their hands, the familiarity of their embrace. I know what they like to eat, their tastes in music, what scenery and art they enjoy—all physical and material things. Ideas are communicated and expressed according to what we can hear, see, taste, touch, and feel. The spiritual and emotional, the intellectual and rational—all find expression through the physical. This is what makes communication with one who is blind, deaf, and mute so very difficult; our common ground in the physical world is severely limited. We underemphasize the physical and take it for granted precisely because it is so ubiquitous.

Similarly much of our knowledge of God comes through the physical world. The Incarnation is the supreme example of this— God taking the form of man in order to reveal Himself to us. Even before this, however, God's communication and appearances to man were by means of the material world. He appeared to Moses in a burning bush; He showed Himself to the children of Israel in a pillar of cloud and a pillar of fire; He gave the Israelites directions to make a visible tabernacle for Him and promised to "dwell" there; He spoke in an audible voice. When He gave commandments, they were precise and concrete; when He demanded worship, it was according to a prescribed ritual; when He desired a tabernacle, He gave exact directions regarding its construction and furnishings.

The worship God required involved using the physical senses: Incense and the smell of animal sacrifices; hangings of red and purple, embroidered with gold; bells on the priestly robes, and trumpets for announcements and summonses. God gave His people the means to worship Him, ways to follow His laws, and reminders of His past working—all involving the physical, material world. Sacrifices entailed specified animals and precise measurements of wine, oil, and flour; feasts included the ritual of washing, clean clothes, and special foods. Ritual words, repeated in poetry and song, marked the various yearly festivals. The Old Testament is replete with the use of the material world, both as a reminder of the greatness and goodness of God and as a means to worship Him.

Unless we see ourselves as an integrated blend, an astonishing union of body, soul, and spirit, we cannot apprehend the biblical meaning of death. In our very being the spiritual and material are as inextricably mixed as they are in the Old Testament pattern of the revelation of God to His people and their worship of Him. With the creation of man as a physical being, God gave meaning and sanctity to the physical universe; with the Incarnation, God affirmed the sanctity of the physical body of man and of the natural world; the resurrection of Christ is the crowning affirmation of the sanctity and value of the created universe. If we are intended to be a divine integration of the physical and spiritual, then death is the unnatural and lamented division of that which should not be divided. The Resurrection becomes the natural end of man, not physical death.

In this view of man, death cannot be denied or approached as something unreal or unimportant. The essential person is not, as we sometimes believe, a soul and spirit, but rather the undivided, integrated unit of body, soul, and spirit.

FACING UP TO DEATH

It is natural to avoid and deny death. Loss, grief, and the stark outrage that we feel in the face of death are uncomfortable, disturbing emotions. We would prefer to accept death as a friend, as the natural end of all created beings, as a welcome end to the hindrances and handicaps of our physical nature. Rather than attempting to find peace in the midst of loss, or meaning in the experience of chaos, we try to avoid the disagreeable and hurtful aspects of death by denying or suppressing the physical, emotional side of ourselves.

We immediately run into a problem when we attempt to use Scripture in "spiritualizing" death. Paul clearly refers to death as an enemy, and he is only one of many biblical writers who refer to death this way.

The final validation of the physical universe and the meaning of man as body, soul, and spirit lies in the Incarnation and the Resurrection. If the body is truly an inconvenience, a hindrance, an embarrassment that we would be better off without, then the Resurrection makes no sense. There could be no conceivable reason for the purified spirit and soul of Christ, freed at last from the body at the Crucifixion, to involve itself again with a body in the Resurrection. Yet we believe in the actual, physical, bodily resurrection of Christ. We have evidence that this body was visible, tangible, audible: He spoke, walked, ate, and prayed with His followers after His resurrection. In His resurrection Christ assumed a permanent involvement with the physical world and, by the transformation of His own body through His victory over death, gave a foretaste of the meaning of God's promise of renewal for all creation.

The appearance of Christ among His followers in a resurrection body affirms the true nature of man as a paradox. Just as God is Three-in-One, just as Christ is God-man, so too is man body-soul-spirit. He is by nature a mystery and a paradox: An animal body possessed of a rational faculty and an immortal soul; an immortal spirit expressed in mind, emotions, will, and body.

THE HOPE OF RESURRECTION

This is where the Christian definition of death begins. If man is truly an integrated union of body, soul, and spirit, then death is an unnatural division of that which ought not to be divided. It is an

167

enemy and a destroyer. Only in light of this approach to death do the resurrection of Christ and the promise of resurrection for His followers attain their full significance.

Death, then, is a division in the very nature of man. Because of this, it also separates man, if only temporarily, from the totality of the created world. When the spiritual part of man is separated from the physical, a person loses contact with and enjoyment of things physical. Because we know each other and communicate by means of the physical world, it also brings separation from those we know and love.

When I die, I will no longer be able to see my children's faces or feel their kisses. I will no longer drive my car, play the piano, sleep in my bed. I will no longer feel the warmth of the sun on my body, shiver in the cold, or get the ache in my back that comes from sitting too long. I will no longer be a part of this physical world, and I will lose all that it holds for me.

Thanks to Jesus Christ, this separation from my body, my loved ones, and the created world need not be permanent. Thanks also to Him, I need never experience enduring separation from God.

Like so many other things in Scripture, death itself is a paradox. Although all the above is true, there are times and ways in this fallen and sin-tainted world in which our enemy death can be a friend. It is, now, the expected and normal end of all life. In the ravages of illness or the steady decline of age, it can become a welcome release from the laws of deterioration and corruption that now govern our fallen world. Paul—the same Paul who describes death as an enemy—expresses this dilemma more than once. In Philippians 1:23 he says, "I am torn between the two: I desire to depart and be with Christ, which is better by far; but it is more necessary for you that I remain in the body." In 2 Corinthians 5:6–8 he states, "As long as we are at home in the body we are away from the Lord. We live by faith, not by sight. We are confident, I say, and would prefer to be away from the body and at home with the Lord."

These last words are preceded by the following: "Now we know that if the earthly tent we live in is destroyed, we have a building from God, an eternal house in heaven, not built by human hands. . . . We do not wish to be unclothed but to be clothed with our heavenly dwelling, so that what is mortal may be swallowed up by life" (2 Cor. 5:1, 4b). The Christian's welcoming of death is never just for the sake of death itself; it has the Resurrection in view. "Putting off this mortal body" has the purpose to be clothed with the spiritual body that shall be ours. Even as an enemy, death has been transformed by the resurrection of Christ, which holds for us too the promise of resurrection. This is the hope in which we are saved, the redemption of the body spoken of by Paul in Romans 8.

So the Christian view of death is twofold. On the one hand, it is an enemy, destroying man, tearing apart families, leaving friends bereft. On the other hand, it is a friend, ending the suffering, debilitation, and limitations imposed on us by our fallen physical bodies and opening up the way for us to be "fully clothed" in a spiritual, resurrection body like that of our risen Lord.

The teaching of the Resurrection makes reconciliation possible between these two aspects of death. Paul says, "If only for this life we have hope in Christ, we are to be pitied more than all men" (1 Cor. 15:19). He says this, asserting that the resurrection of Jesus Christ is the cornerstone of the Christian faith. Only by a physical, bodily resurrection could Christ finally undo the destruction of death and wholly remake fallen man in His own image, the image of God. Man without a body is incomplete; he is not man as God created him in the beginning, nor man as God has re-created him in Christ.

The teaching of the Resurrection gives hope to our mourning and brings light into the darkness of our grief. Christ has reversed the effects of the Fall and the separation brought about by disobedience. He has reunited man to God, man to man, and man to himself. Finally the entire created world will be redeemed, "liberated from its bondage to decay and brought into the glorious freedom of the children of God" (Rom. 8:21).

Thus, death the destroyer has been transformed into the gateway to eternity, the door from our present exile from Christ in this body into our home with Him. "Then the saying that is written will come true: 'Death has been swallowed up in victory'" (1 Cor. 15:54).

APPENDIX 2
SUICIDE AND
CHRISTIAN TEACHING

THE THOUGHT OF SUICIDE brings shock and horror. Why would anyone want to end his own life? What brings a person to such a desperate act?

Unless it is forced upon our attention, suicide is very likely something we avoid thinking and talking about. We try to ignore the fact that suicides occur. Yet suicide is one of the leading causes of death among young people in the United States and the statistics seem to be rising. But suicide statistics, as shocking and frightening as they are, are only the "tip of the iceberg"; they include only known suicides and do not account for some suicides that are reported as accidents, cases in which suicide is suspected but not proved, or the many unsuccessful suicide attempts.

In the climate of our society we can no longer continue to ignore suicide. It is not the rarity we would like to believe it is. It is becoming more and more a considered option and is even gaining a degree of respectability. There are organizations advocating the right of an individual to take his own life; there are even "how-to" books to help the would-be suicide choose the most effective way of killing himself! More and more people of all ages and in all circumstances think about suicide at one time or another in their lives; this includes young adults, teen-agers, and even children.

As evidence of the idea that even children think about suicide, I need only to look at my own son, Jimmy. Jimmy and I took a walk one beautiful, sunny day. Spring was in full bloom. The crocuses had faded and died, but the tulips and daffodils still held their blossoms proudly tall. The flowering crabs, the redbuds, and magnolia lent softness, color, and fragrance to the sky. The sun was warm, the breeze was chill, and the birds were singing. In the middle of all this, my five-year-old son turned to me and said, "Mommy, I wish I could die!"

"Why in the world would you want to die? Look at the beautiful world around us; why would you want to leave it?"

"I don't like this world. It has tornadoes and hurricanes. There are storms and floods. People get hurt and get killed. Why did God make a world like this?"

Jimmy has long been aware of the dual nature of creation—its beauty, joy, and laughter; its destruction, fear, and horror. Fall and winter follow every summer; the most beautiful summer day can quickly yield to a frightening thunderstorm; the spring flowers already carry the beginning of their own death. We are powerless in the face of the fury of a tornado, a raging flood, or a howling windstorm. Horror and destruction can take over our day, and we are powerless to stop it or even to understand it. Nature is capricious, smiling on us one minute and frowning the next. Without warning, natural forces can sweep away all we care about and have worked for, all our dreams and plans; this destruction is meaningless and random.

I can identify with Jimmy's feelings and his statement. I too have rebelled at living in a world where sixty-mile-an-hour winds can obliterate the hard work of many years, where the twenty-six-year-old mother of two toddlers can get leukemia and die within six weeks, where men and women can be treated as objects and become pawns in the power struggle between opposing political groups. Sometimes I feel like telling God, "If this is the best You can do with this world, count me out! I refuse to participate in Your creation if You can't manage it any better than this!"

THE FRAME OF MIND

Usually these feelings are momentary and pass. Often they are accompanied by other signs and feelings of depression. Yet there are times in the lives of many when the desperation and hopelessness of personal life seem echoed in the meaninglessness and absurdity of the universe, and the only sensible solution seems to be to end it all—to die and be rid once for all of problems, frustrations, helplessness, and despair.

The person who chooses suicide is generally in this frame of mind. Everything is hopeless, out of control, and in a mess. His personal life seems futile and useless, without meaning or direction; the world itself is a confusing mixture of good and bad, with the bad seeming to overpower and outweigh the good. Suicide seems the only possible solution, a lone sane act in an insane world.

In my opinion, suicide is always a decision reached in an "unsound mind." It is an expression of acute mental anguish. It is a distortion and misapprehension of facts. The weight of despair is so heavy that no gleam of hope or possibility of change can be felt or even imagined by the person. It often represents a tension between the feelings "I'm no good, and everyone would be better off without me" and "I don't deserve to suffer like this, and I can't stand it any longer."

Suicide is a final, violent protest by an individual—a protest against anonymity, against meaninglessness and absurdity in his life and his universe, against frustration, helplessness, and loss of control. It is an attempt to regain control in some way; it is an attempt "to take arms against a sea of troubles, And by opposing end them" (Hamlet's Soliloquy). It can also be an angry statement roughly equivalent to the child playing ball who says, "If you won't play my way, I'll just take my ball and go home!" At times there may be a component of revenge in the suicide: "When I'm dead and gone, *then* you'll be sorry!"

Suicidal thoughts are frequently a part of severe depression. Both depression and the thoughts of suicide may recur in some people. Jimmy's expression, "I wish I could die," has been uttered at times other than that springtime walk with me; he has even asked *how* he could kill himself. (I have told him very firmly that this is information I refuse to give him in that I believe it would be dangerous to him!) Some people are more prone than others to consider suicide because of their tendency to depression; this tendency also shows some evidence of running in families, possibly being an inherited trait.

THE SCRIPTURAL VIEW

I am utterly appalled by some of the current attempts to make suicide an acceptable option, even a "reasonable" choice. This view necessarily accepts the suicidal person's view of the world and his own life as meaningless, hopeless, and absurd; it agrees with him that this is the "only way out" of a situation.

This is completely opposed to the scriptural view of the world, man, and God. The Bible responds to the suicidal person by saying, "Hang in there! There's hope for you and for the world as well." God is presented in Scripture as the Author and Giver of life, its Sustainer, and the One who determines its longevity. Scripture also offers many examples and statements that indicate there is a meaningful universe, plan, and design in a person's life and value and purpose even in experiences of pain, anguish, and suffering. The Bible repudiates the statement, "I can't take any more, so I'm going to end it all," with the assurance that God never allows us more difficulty or trouble than we can bear and that He Himself can and will provide us with grace and strength to endure.

Although I know of no place in the Bible where suicide as a particular instance of killing is specifically prohibited, the body of scriptural teaching opposes the view that it is an option for the Christian. This interpretation of the biblical message has its roots in Judaism and is continued throughout the history of the Christian church. God is in charge of His creation. He brings rains and springs of water to nourish the grass and the trees; He provides food for the beasts of the field, and gives them life or takes it away (Pss. 103, 104); He has known us from the moment of our conception, and we are made according to His plan (Ps. 139:13, 15–16), a knowledge that includes our psychological and emotional make-up as well as our physical bodies; He knows us intimately, even knowing what we will do or say before we have done or said it (Ps. 139:1–6). There is nowhere we can hide from God or be hidden from His view, His love, and His care (Ps. 139:7–12); and our death is precious in the sight of the Lord (Ps. 116:15). Children of God, born into His family by faith in Jesus Christ, are addressed even more specifically in terms of His plans and purposes. He has known us and predestined us to be conformed to the image of His Son (Rom. 8:29); we are His workmanship, and He has created us for good works, prepared beforehand for us to walk in (Eph. 2:10). Furthermore, the feeling and belief that suicide is the "only way out" is contradicted in 1 Corinthians 10:13, where we are clearly told that God has provided a way of escape from our temptations, a way that will make them bearable.

The psalmists give ample testimony to feelings of depression and worthlessness, yet most of these same psalms end with a statement of trust in God and often also of praise to Him. Time and again God is described as Keeper as well as Savior; He is our Deliverer from our enemies, including the enemy named Depression. If, as Jesus says, the very hairs of our head are numbered (Matt. 10:30), then it is unreasonable to suppose that God does not know the length of our life and our suffering. Suicide implies that God has forgotten about me, allowed me to live too long, or suffer too much; since God is no longer keeping track of my days and my hours, I must take matters into my own hands. This is totally contrary to the biblical emphasis of trust in God regardless of our circumstances or our feelings about them. As I read it, the biblical message to the depressed or suicidal person can be summarized, "Hang in there! Help is on the way!"

FORMS OF SUICIDE

The word *suicide* in general means the deliberate ending (or attempt to end) one's own life. I find it helpful to differentiate active suicide, suicide attempts, and passive suicide.

"Active suicide" is a deliberate decision to end one's life and taking a definite course of action to accomplish this. The "suicide attempt" may be the same as active suicide, except that the intended course of action to end life has been interrupted, has miscarried, or has been reversed by the intervention of others. At other times there is ambivalence toward the decision to commit suicide; unconsciously the person himself "arranges" to be found in time or to be interrupted in his attempt. The suicide attempt, in any event, is a desperate cry for help.

The act of suicide or the suicide attempt does not usually arise from a sudden decision. It is generally the product of a long period of depression or repeated depressions. Over a period of time the person begins to feel more and more hopeless. At some point the thought takes root that he would be better off dead and that others might be better off without him. As this thought is entertained and encouraged, the thought of suicide occurs. At first this may be an "emergency" measure—an escape route only if things "get too bad." Initially the thought is probably accompanied by revulsion and the feeling that "I wouldn't ever *really* do it."

However, if the depression continues, the feelings of worthlessness and inadequacy grow, frustrations multiply, and the person is overwhelmed by fatigue and a sense of futility. His mind turns again to the thought of suicide, and he moves on to planning.

Plans to commit suicide are not definite and real at first. They take the form of a mental exercise: "If I decided to commit suicide, how would I do it?" If the depression continues and the person still entertains the thought of suicide, he eventually evolves a plan: "If I were going to commit suicide, I would. . . ." In time, these thoughts become a habit and even an obsession. Plans become more concrete, and the person may even start preparing to fulfill them. At some point an attempt is made.

The success of the attempt depends partly on the degree of ambivalence the person feels about his decision and partly on circumstances. If the person has a deep, unconscious desire to live, his attempt is more likely to fail than succeed; if he is fortunate, the suicide attempt will bring him to the help he has called out for in such a dramatic way.

Even though not every suicide attempt succeeds, the conscious intention is fatal. There is at least some part of the person's mind and will that wishes to see life end. This may be countered by another part of the mind and will that hopes he will be found "in time" and spared from death. In fact, I believe that most people wish that someone would help them find an alternative, a way out of the blackness and despair, a method to make life meaningful, tolerable, or even enjoyable.

"Passive Suicide"

"Passive suicide" is more complex and more difficult to deal with than active suicide. A person may not consciously want to die, yet he will engage in activities and a lifestyle that hold a high statistical probability of shortening one's life without resulting in immediate death. Some examples are overworking, overeating, drinking or smoking too much, neglecting to take necessary medication for blood pressure or heart disease or another chronic ailment, living a life of stress, and neglecting physical exercise.

These "passive" measures are not quite the same as overt suicidal action. Careless driving, lack of exercise, overwork, and the other measures are all gambles. They may result in death or disability (and it is fairly likely that they will), yet there is a chance that they will not. In many cases, the motivation for such behavior is the same as in overt suicidal attempts, although the wish to die is usually unconscious.

A person who indulges in behavior that has a high probability of shortening his life may in fact despise his life. He may have a basic feeling of worthlessness. He may consider what he can "accomplish" by his unhealthy lifestyle of more value than the life it jeopardizes. He may also use these behaviors and activities as an escape from himself, a barrier between him and a knowledge of himself as God created him and desires him to be.

The passive suicide is also acting out of a measure of rebellion against God and the universe. He refuses to accept and submit to the laws of nature and the laws of his own body. Thus he neglects the legitimate needs of his body for rest, exercise, proper diet, and recreation and indulges in activities that have a high probability of being harmful. Instead of being characterized by the statement, "If you won't play my way, I'll take my ball and go home," he is more accurately portrayed by the statement, "You play by your rules, but I'll play by mine as long as I can, and if I get caught, I get caught!"

The person with passive suicidal behavior may have low self-esteem, a sense of worthlessness and guilt. Some behavior may be designed to make up for his feelings of worthlessness. His drive may be intended to prove his worth to himself and to others. His feelings of lack of worth and of hopelessness may not be evident to others and may completely contradict the facts as others see them. Many of these people hold a place of prominence or esteem, are considered a success by peers and acquaintances, and seem externally to "have it made."

Denying Life-Support

One other circumstance that has recently come to be included with passive suicide is the denial of life-support measures to a person who is terminally ill.

The life-support measures in view are those designed only to support and prolong life. They are not envisioned as a cure for the patient's basic illness; they serve mainly to give him more time. If this time will allow further treatment of the underlying disease, and if there is a reasonable expectation that the disease will respond to the treatment, then I believe life-sustaining measures can be justified. In the patient with leukemia, there are times during initial treatment when life must be supported by transfusions, antibiotics, and other aggressive care to give the anti-leukemia drugs time to work and the body a chance to respond to them. If the patient develops pneumonia at this stage, it makes good sense to treat the pneumonia promptly and aggressively. Intensive life-support measures taken to make transplantation a possibility for a person in kidney failure, with all its complications, also falls into this category.

Perhaps, however, the person who suffers a heart attack already has lung cancer that is too advanced for surgery and does not respond to chemotherapy or radiation. Resuscitation is an option that this person has every reason to refuse. In the same way, if a patient develops pneumonia during the fourth or fifth course of unsuccessful treatment for leukemia, his choice to refuse treatment for the pneumonia is reasonable. In these instances, the refusal of life-support measures may be better regarded as a refusal to deny the seriousness of the underlying illness than as a form of "passive suicide."

When a person has an illness for which there is no therapy with a reasonable (at least 50 percent) likelihood of cure or remission, the acceptance or refusal of medical treatment needs to be made in the context of his total life and his priorities for the rest of his life. In this situation, refusing treatment that is aimed solely at prolonging life is quite different from the deliberate act of ending a life, or even from indulging in habits of behavior that are likely to shorten a life. Personally I cannot find a reason why refusal of life-support in this situation should be classed as suicide, even of the "passive" form.

ETERNAL DESTINY

The question arises of the eternal destiny of one who chooses to end his own life and succeeds. We have already defined suicide as an act expressing a weakness of faith in God, at the very least, or an act of deliberate defiance against God. Is it, then, an unpardonable sin? Does it necessarily mean a denial of faith, a turning of one's back on God, a repudiation of one's position as a child of God?

Suicide is a desperate, violent, and sometimes angry refusal of

God's gift of life. It usurps God's prerogative to determine the issues of life and death; it is an act of pride and rebellion in that it refuses to let God be God. As such, it is a sin.

However, refusing the gift of life occurs on many levels; the sin of pride can take many forms. Many activities, compulsions, and indulgences involve neglecting or despising the body and, as such, they are refusals of God's gift of life. Some of these have been discussed as forms of passive suicide. Although the outcome of these acts is not as sudden or as certain as the deliberate, active suicide, these seem to me to fall into the same category both morally and theologically. If we are not prepared to say that *these* sins can deny our redemption to God in Christ Jesus (assuming that we already have saving faith in Him) I believe we should not be too quick to say that suicide itself can damn us either.

Our redemption is a gift. Our salvation is free, paid for by God, not by our good deeds or good intentions either before our receiving it or after. The fact that we are sinners is not changed by our behavior; our behavior changes in response to our redemption. Furthermore, the Christian life is a life of continual growth and progress. It involves increasing awareness of who God is, who we are in relation to Him, and the grace and mandate inherent in His choosing us.

Paul says to the Galatians, and to us, "Did you receive the Spirit by observing the law, or by believing what you heard? Are you so foolish? After beginning with the Spirit, are you now trying to attain your goals by human effort? Have you suffered so much for nothing—if it really was for nothing? Does God give you his Spirit and work miracles among you because you observe the law, or because you believe what you heard?" (Gal. 3:2b—5). It seems clear that maintaining and growing in the faith of our Lord Jesus Christ is the prerequisite for Christian growth, and the works follow after the faith.

Actions and attitudes proceed from our level of maturity in faith. As young Christians we may have certain attitudes and cling to certain actions that we later abandon. We may also find certain Christlike behavior and attitudes impossible to us until we come to greater maturity in our faith. Paul speaks to this in Romans 14, explaining that in some matters of attitude and conduct the definition of sin depends on our faith and our maturity of faith.

Obviously the question of losing one's faith arises. However, this is different from the question as to whether a single sin—even deliberate and premeditated—can destroy our salvation. The point is made throughout the New Testament that those who are born of God do not continue living in sin. It is also implicit, however, that God's children—living by faith, being conformed more and more to the image of Christ by the work of the Holy Spirit and the surrender of their own will—do commit sin. Provision is made for that sin through repentance, confession, and forgiveness on the basis of Christ's atoning work on the cross (1 John 1:9). It seems to me that there is no New Testament case for stating that a single sin can automatically result in the loss of our salvation. I believe that this extends to the matter of suicide.

For some, 1 John 5:16–17 poses a problem in this regard. These verses state, "If anyone sees his brother commit a sin that does not lead to death ["not a mortal sin"—Revised Standard Version], he should pray and God will give him life. I refer to those whose sin does not lead to death. There is a sin that leads to death. I am not saying that he should pray about that. All wrongdoing is sin, and there is sin that does not lead to death." Although many commentators view the "mortal sin" as apostasy, and the death described as spiritual, I believe there is another possible explanation. Mortal sin is that sin which as its natural outcome results in physical death. It seems clear to me in the context of the New Testament that the only sin that brings damnation is the sin of unbelief in the atonement of Jesus Christ. The context in 1 John concerns a "brother," which seems to refer to a fellow-believer, someone who is born anew into God's family by faith in Christ. Therefore the mortal sin referred to cannot be the sin of unbelief. There are sinful actions on our part that can result in our physical death, and I believe that this is what is meant in these verses.

The more difficult question of loss of faith is one I cannot deal with here. There are able contenders with good scriptural arguments on both sides of this issue. I wish only to state that I believe it is possible to commit suicide in a "state of faith," just as it is possible to commit adultery or steal or lie or gossip or indulge in self-righteousness while in a "state of faith." Of course, interesting as it is in the abstract, the matter of the eternal destiny of one who commits suicide becomes vitally important when we are faced with the suicide of a friend. I have offered these comments, as my understanding of the Scriptures, in the hope that they may be helpful.

Time for Reconciliation

There is one further issue to raise in regard to suicide. In the event of instant death, it is hard to imagine time or opportunity for repentance and forgiveness. However, during an interval between the suicidal act and death, even in a condition of coma or unconsciousness, there is time for reconciliation with God. Our increasing knowledge of unconscious states suggests that the lack of consciousness is more a matter of lack of outward communication with the environment than necessarily a state of unawareness, mindlessness, or the cessation of spiritual, emotional, and mental activity. Those who have recovered from unconscious states report being aware of what was going on around them, of hearing and seeing people who were with them. It is not inconceivable that spiritual and intellectual activity can continue in one who is unconscious.

Therefore it is possible to believe that even the suicide, in the moments between his act and his death, can experience repentance, forgiveness, and reconciliation with God in accordance with 1 John 1:9. We dare not forget that God is exceedingly merciful and well aware of our failings and frailties. Remember that Christ came into the world to offer salvation, not to bring condemnation (John 3:17).

In conclusion, suicide is sin. However, our God forgives sins. As humans we tend to arrange sins in an orderly fashion, progressing from the "least sinful" to the "most sinful." Even if there is a legitimate distinction between the "sinfulness" of different sins, I am inclined to believe that it does not always agree with our carefully ordered hierarchy. I believe God takes into account the full circumstances surrounding a sinful act, and His judgment of us is always liberally mixed with His mercy and His grace. He is more willing to forgive us than we are to forgive ourselves; He is more willing to accept and allow for our frailties and failings than we are. We must remember that the atonement of Christ covers all sins. In the final analysis, in this situation (as in all others) we must fall back on our trust in God and our belief in His infinite goodness, mercy, and love toward His own.

181

BIBLIOGRAPHY

Bernstein, Joanne E., comp. *Books to Help Children Cope With Separation and Loss.* New York: R. R. Bowker, 1977.

This is a listing of literature available to help children cope with grief. An introductory section explains how parents and teachers can use books effectively in dealing with children. The listing is divided according to types of losses and covers such topics as adoption, divorce, moving, and death. It leans heavily on fictional representations of separation and loss. It is weak on religious fiction and presentations of Christian answers to grief. However, it is an excellent resource for books that can be read to and by children to help them understand grief.

BOOKS FOR CHILDREN

Bernstein, Joanne E. *Loss and How to Cope With It.* Boston: Houghton Mifflin, 1981.

Use with children grades 6 and up.

Bernstein, Joanne E., and Stephen V. Gullo. *When People Die.* Photographs by Rosemarie Hauscherr. New York: E. P. Dutton, 1977.

Use with children kindergarten through grade 3.

L'Engle, Madeleine. *Camilla: A Novel.* New York: Dell, 1982.

Grades 7 and up. Deals with divorce, depression, alcoholism, death, separation from friends and family. Suggest parents read first; may be too "heavy" for some young teens.

_____. *Dragons in the Waters*. New York: Dell, 1982.

Ages 10 and up. Deals with the death of both parents (preceding the beginning of the story), the death of a pet, the death of an ideal, murder, the terminal illness of a grandmother. Presents a compassionate, humane approach to terminal illness, and a new perspective on the art of healing. Solid Christian approach, avoiding pat answers.

_____. *Meet the Austins*. New York: Dell, 1981.

Ages 10 and up. Deals with the death of a good friend and the only remaining parent of a young girl. Realistic picture of the grief of a young child and its varied expressions. Solid Christian approach.

_____. *A Ring of Endless Light*. New York: Dell, 1982.

Ages 10 and up. Deals with the death of parents (of two different young men) and two different reactions to their deaths, an attempted suicide, and the progressive, terminal leukemia of the grandfather. Main character is a sixteen-year-old girl; easy to identify with. Solid Christian approach, avoiding pat answers.

_____. *The Young Unicorns*. New York: Dell, 1980.

Ages 10 and up. Deals with the loss of sight of a young girl. Grief handled sensitively and realistically. Parents should read first, as it may be too "heavy" for some young people.

Lewis, C. S. *The Last Battle*. The Chronicles of Narnia. New York: Macmillan, 1970.

Ages 6 and up. Deals with the "new heaven and new earth" idea. Parent should read first, as some ideas presented are a slight departure from standard evangelical teachings.

_____. *The Lion, the Witch and the Wardrobe*. The Chronicles of Narnia. New York: Macmillan, 1970.

Ages 6 and up. Deals with the Crucifixion and Resurrection metaphorically. Excellent for catching the feelings of grief and loss at death, and the joy and exhilaration of the Resurrection

_____. *The Silver Chair*. The Chronicles of Narnia. New York: Macmillan, 1970.

Ages 6 and up. Deals briefly at the end of the book with what happens to the soul, or spirit, when a person dies, and the concept of the resurrection body.

BOOKS FOR PARENTS

Bayly, Joseph T. _____. *The Last Thing We Talk About*. Elgin, Ill.: David C. Cook, 1973.

Personal account of the loss of three children. Formerly entitled *The View From a Hearse*.

Grollman, Earl A. *Explaining Death to Children*. Boston: Beacon Press, 1969.

_____. *Talking About Death: A Dialogue Between Parent and Child*, With Parent's Guide and Recommended Resources. Boston: Beacon Press, 1976.

For use with children kindergarten through grade 4.

Jackson, Edgar N. *The Many Faces of Grief*. Nashville: Abingdon, 1977.

_____. *Telling a Child About Death*. New York: E. P. Dutton, 1965.

_____. *Understanding Grief*. Nashville: Abingdon, 1957.

Lewis, C. S. *A Grief Observed*. New York: Bantam, 1976.

Morris, Sarah M. *Grief and How to Live With It*. New York: Grossett and Dunlap, Family Inspirational Library, 1972.

Robinson, Haddon W. *Grief*. Grand Rapids: Zondervan, 1976.

Tanner, Ira J. *Healing the Pain of Everyday Loss*. Minneapolis: Winston, 1980.

INDEX

Mommy, What Does It Mean To Die?

Juanita and Jim Kopp,
With Their Mother

A LETTER TO PARENTS

THE FOLLOWING PAGES are intended to be read by you and your child together. They may be read aloud to a five-to-seven-year-old, or read individually by you and an older child, then discussed. The material is not intended to replace discussion between you and your child about death, but rather to stimulate the discussion and provide a springboard for more detailed conversations.

This section covers the most common, basic questions children ask about death. Although it provides some answers, it is not the final word on their questions. The answers here reflect conventional Christian teaching; because there is disagreement among sincere believers on some of the basic points, my approach to most topics is general and should allow you to interpret these truths according to your own beliefs and the teachings of your church.

We suggest that you use this section in this way: Chapter headings take the form of questions, and some chapters begin with a series of questions relating to a child's world and experience. While reading with a child, allow him to answer the questions before continuing with the text. Allow time to discuss any question that arouses your child's interest. At the end of each chapter there are additional questions for continuing the discussion. Most of these questions are designed so that there are not "right" or "wrong" answers; they relate to thoughts, memories, experiences, and feelings.

A child's attention span may be short. He may wish to end the discussion before a chapter has been completed; some chapters may arouse no interest in him, or he may wish to skip around and not read them in the order in which they are presented. It is best to follow a child's own interests and inclinations, as he will learn better and remember more on a topic that interests him. Use the material as a reference; be willing to abandon it for a time and return to it later, prompted by your child's readiness to stop or continue.

Most of the material presented in this section comes directly from conversations between my children and me—conversations ranging over the years when they were aged three to ten. We have not yet reached the end of our own discussions; some questions presented here have been answered for us in different ways at different times. It is my hope and prayer that these conversations regarding grief and death will be as helpful to you and your children as they have been to me and mine.

Ruth Kopp, M.D.

WHAT DOES "DEAD" MEAN?

HAVE YOU EVER "played dead"? Do you ever play cowboys and Indians, Space Invaders, cops and robbers, or other games with shooting and killing? What happens if you are "shot dead" in a game?

Have you ever seen someone die on television or in a movie? Can you remember what happens? I can remember watching the Lone Ranger on TV. When a "bad guy" got shot, he would grab his chest with a hand, fall off his horse, roll over one or two times on the ground, and then lie still. A crowd would come up and look at the dead man, then several men would pick him up by his feet and his shoulders and carry him off. I'd never see him again on that program.

Have you ever seen a dead animal? Have you come close to it, looked at it, and maybe even touched it? Sometimes there is a dead bird on my lawn. Sometimes I pass a dead squirrel or rabbit in the road. We have had pets that died —fish, chameleons, snakes. A dead animal looks and feels and acts different from a living one. A dead bird looks funny: It lies there, still, stiff, not moving. Its eyes might be open and still. It can't get up and hop away or fly into a tree. If you touch it, it feels hard and cold. A dead fish doesn't swim with the other fish: It floats on top of the aquarium. Its pretty colors are gone, and it looks dull.

There was a sick horse at the stable where we have our

horses. When he was sick, he could walk around slowly and eat. When flies landed on him, he swished his tail and twitched his skin to get rid of them. He turned his head when he heard us coming, or when we called his name. When he was lying down asleep, his sides went up and down with his breathing.

This horse didn't get well. Even though the vet gave him medicine, he died. When he was dead, he was lying on his side in his stall. His sides didn't go up and down anymore, because he wasn't breathing When flies landed on him, he didn't swish his tail or twitch his skin. When we walked up to him and called his name, he didn't turn his head or move at all.

Plants can die too. Some plants are weeds, and we are glad when they die. We pull them out of the garden Pretty soon they look all withered and shriveled up. Their leaves turn yellow, brown, or black. They don't get any new leaves or flowers.

People can die too. When a person is dead, he doesn't eat or drink or talk anymore. His heart stops beating and he stops breathing. He can't hear or see, taste or touch anymore. A dead person is not asleep, because he doesn't move, breathe, dream, or hear the way a sleeping person does.

QUESTIONS

1. What can living things do that dead things can't do?
2. How is being dead different from playing dead?
3. How is being dead different from being asleep?
4. Why do people sometimes say that being dead is like being asleep? Is it?
5. How is being dead in real life different from being dead in a movie or on TV?

WHAT AND WHO CAN DIE?

To DIE MEANS to stop being alive, so something must be alive before it can die. Things that aren't alive can't die. In the beginning, when God made the world, He made many, many things. He made the sun, the moon, the stars, the rocks, and the rivers; these things were not alive. He also made many, many living things of different kinds: Plants, like roses and oak trees, apple trees and daffodils, Christmas trees and raspberry bushes; animals, like elephants and rabbits, whales and guppies, dogs and tigers, horses and skunks. The living things could eat and drink and grow; they could also 'reproduce,' that is, make new living things of their same kind. Rabbits have baby bunnies; oak trees make acorns, from which new oak trees can grow; guppies have baby guppies, and the apple seeds inside the apples can grow new apple trees.

After God made the world, the plants, and the animals, He made mankind. He made a man and a woman, and they too were living. They ate and drank, grew and slept, and later on had babies. God made man different from the other animals, though: God made man to be like Him. This means, among other things, that man can also make things. He can make buildings, cars, vacuum cleaners, typewriters, dolls, and trains. But man cannot give life to the things he makes; only God can do that.

In our world now there are many things that are living and many things that are not living. Plants and animals and people are the living things; stones, buildings, machines, toys, rocks, and oceans are not living. Only the things that are living can die.

When God first made the world, there was no dying. There was no sickness, no killing. After God had made the world, He made a special garden for the man and woman to live in, and He told Adam and Eve to take care of the other living things and rule over them. He also told them that they could use the fruit from the trees for their food—all except for one tree. There was one kind of fruit God told them not to eat.

Eve was tricked. She did what God told her not to do and ate the fruit that God had forbidden. After she disobeyed, she told Adam what she had done, and Adam disobeyed God too.

God had warned Adam and Eve that if they disobeyed Him they would die. Disobeying God is sin, the Bible tells us, and when Adam and Eve disobeyed God, sin came into the world. Sin brought sickness and killing and dying into our world. Ever since Adam and Eve, every living thing can die.

Plants are living things. They get food from the ground; they breathe the air; they need water; they grow and make seeds that can make new plants like them. Plants can die. They die if there isn't enough food in the ground for them, or if they don't get enough water. They die if their roots are pulled up out of the ground that has their food and water in it. Plants can be killed, also, by people or animals. Plants can get sick and die of sickness.

Animals are living things. They eat and drink, rest and grow, and have baby animals of their own kind. They too can die. Sometimes they live a long time, and they die because their bodies get old and worn out. Sometimes they get sick and die because of a sickness. Sometimes they get killed in an accident, or other animals or people kill them on purpose.

People are living things too. They eat, drink, grow, sleep, and have babies. Because they are living things, people can die too. Sometimes they get old, and their bodies wear out and they die. Sometimes they get sick, and the doctors, nurses, and medicines can't make them well. People can be killed too. Sometimes they are killed in a car accident, a fire, a flood, or an earthquake. Sometimes animals kill people. Sometimes people even kill other people, or people kill themselves.

When we think of dying, we usually think of old people or animals. Most people will live a long time. Most babies grow up into little children; little children get bigger and become grownups; the grownups live to be old men and women. If we get a puppy or a kitten, we expect it to grow up into a dog or a cat and live with us for a long time.

Living things—plants, animals, and people—don't always get to grow up and get old before they die. Not only grandmas and grandpas die, but mommies and daddies, brothers and sisters, and even babies can die. Pets die too. Most pets don't live as long as people. A dog might live to be twelve or sixteen years old, but that would be very old for a dog. A horse might live for thirty or thirty-five years before it's old. Mice and hamsters, snakes and chameleons, guppies and other fish don't live very long; if they live for a year or two, they are very old. Even pets don't always get to live long enough to get old; kittens and puppies, baby birds and fish can die too.

QUESTIONS

1. Talk about some living things you know, and some things that are not living. How can you tell the difference between a living thing and something that is not alive?

2. How old do you have to be to die?

3. Do you know of any pets that have died? Were they old?

4. Do you know of any people who have died? How old were they? Were they "old enough" to die?   ·

HOW DO LIVING THINGS DIE?

ALL LIVING THINGS need food, air, and water. If they don't get these things, they die. When we pull weeds out of the ground, they die because we take their roots out of the ground and they can't get their food and water. Sometimes animals and even people die because they can't get enough food to eat or water to drink. People and animals drown in the water if they can't get their heads out into the air and have air to breathe.

People and animals in our world get old. What is "old" for a snake isn't the same as what is "old" for a dog; what is "old" for a horse isn't "old" for an elephant. Each kind of animal has a certain number of years it can be expected to live, if it doesn't get sick or die in an accident.

When people or animals live to be old, there are changes in their bodies. We say that these changes come because of old age. The different parts of the body don't work as well as they used to; the heart and lungs, kidneys and brain, blood vessels and stomach start to "wear out." If enough parts of a person's or animal's body "wear out" and don't work right, then the person or the animal dies. We say that this death was because of old age.

Sometimes people and animals are born with something wrong with their bodies. A baby may be born with a hole in its heart or with something wrong with its stomach or lungs.

Sometimes the baby can be helped by operations or medicines, and he can live to grow up; sometimes there are too many things wrong with the baby's body for operations and medicines to help, and he dies. Sometimes something happens to make a baby be born too soon, before it has grown enough inside its mother. Again, special machines and medicines can sometimes help this baby and it lives to grow up; sometimes the special machines and medicines don't work, and the baby dies.

People, animals, and plants die of sicknesses too. In our world today, there are many, many sicknesses that can be treated and cured. There are medicines for sicknesses that used to kill lots of people and animals. Many people in our world, and especially in our country, get the right kind of food and drink and exercise, so they have strong, healthy bodies that are able to fight against sickness. There are shots and vaccines that many babies and children get to keep them from getting some sicknesses that used to cause death.

Not all sicknesses can be treated and cured, however. Not all people have strong, healthy bodies that can fight against sickness. Sometimes a person will get two or three different sicknesses at once, and even with all the medicine and care he will die of the sicknesses.

There are other things that kill people and other living things too. When there is too much rain or snow, so that rivers flood, people and animals can die in the floods. In some parts of the world there are earthquakes; in some places there are tornadoes or hurricanes.

Accidents kill people and animals too. Sometimes cars, airplanes, or trains crash; sometimes houses or office buildings catch fire.

There are also some very, very sad things in our world. There are wars between people in different countries; there are fights between neighbors or even in families; there are people who hate other people, or want what other people have, so much that they are willing to kill. Wars and fights and killings are all part of the sin in our world.

Maybe the very saddest thing in our world is people who kill themselves. Sometimes a person will get very, very sad and discouraged. He feels that nothing is any use; he feels that he is no good; he begins to believe that things will never change and that he will never feel any better. When a person feels this way, it's a kind of sickness. Some people who feel this way decide that they don't want to live anymore, and they kill themselves.

QUESTIONS

1. What kind of sicknesses do you know about? Can these sicknesses be treated? Can people with these sicknesses get well?

2. Do you think that most people who get sick die or get well?

3. Have you ever had to take a sick pet to the vet? Did the pet get well?

4. What do you know about floods, hurricanes, tornadoes, or earthquakes? Are they likely to happen where we live? Are there things we can do to protect ourselves from them?

5. Do many people die in fires? Do you know how to save yourself in a fire at home? at school? at church?

SUGGESTIONS FOR PARENTS

Children should be aware of the ways in which living things can die, and this is not intended to be a "scare" chapter. Be sure your discussion emphasizes their own safety and the relative rarity of death from illness, accident, or natural disaster in their own area and peer group. This may be a good opportunity to review safety rules, however, and make sure that your children know what you do in the event of fire, accident, or other emergency.

Suicide is a leading cause of death in young adults. As such, it cannot be avoided in this book or in discussion of death with our children. I personally would never tell a child how he could commit suicide even if he asked how. But if a child shows an unusual amount of interest in the question of suicide, you should help him explore his own feelings and find ways of coping with them. For further information on suicide, please refer to the appendixes of this book.

WHAT HAPPENS WHEN PEOPLE DIE?

When God made people, He made them different from other living things. The Bible says that God made people like Him. People are like other animals in that they have bodies which can run and jump, sleep and eat; people are like God because they are more than just bodies. There is a part of each person that can't be seen. The body is the part of us that we see when we look at each other or look into a mirror; the other part of the person—the spirit, or the soul—is the part of us that thinks, feels, loves, hates, gets excited, or gets angry.

We can think about the body and spirit as the clothes a person wears and the person inside. The person inside is the spirit; the clothes he wears are the body. A person can take off his clothes; when someone dies, it's as if the spirit has taken off the clothes that are his body. The clothes are left behind—sometimes in a heap on the floor, sometimes hung up neatly in the closet or draped over a chair—but they are empty. The dead body is like the clothes without the person inside; it can't move or talk or feel anymore. When a person dies, only the body dies. The spirit, or soul, moves out of the body, and it is left like an empty pair of jeans and a shirt.

Sometimes when the body dies, it can be brought back to life. If a person stops breathing or his heart stops beating and there is someone close by who can help the person start breathing again or start his heart beating again, he won't die. The spirit, or soul, can go on living inside that body.

When a person dies and his spirit, or soul, leaves his body, what happens? If the person is a Christian when he dies—that is, if he has asked Jesus to forgive his sins—his spirit, or soul, goes to be with Jesus in heaven. Then his body is buried. But that isn't the end.

Death is a part of the world that we live in now. It came into the world a long, long time ago, when Adam and Eve decided to disobey God. It is still here. However, God has promised that there will be a day when there will be an end to death and to dying. When that day comes, every person who has died will get a new body; the spirit, or soul, will be "dressed" again, in a new suit of clothes.

Many people have wondered about this new body. Many people have had many ideas and have even written books about it. God hasn't told us very much about it in the Bible. I think He's keeping it for us, like an extraspecial present, until the day comes.

We know that Jesus died. His spirit, or soul, went away from His body. His body was buried in a tomb. When Jesus rose from the dead, He had a new body, the kind of new body that we are going to have. If we think what Jesus was like after He rose from the dead, we can get a few ideas of what our new bodies will be like.

What was Jesus' new body like? It was a body that His disciples could recognize, but they couldn't always recognize it right away. It was a body that did the things our bodies do: He walked with His disciples, He talked with them, He held bread in His hands, He ate, He cooked fish, He could be touched and handled. His new body even had the scars from the nails and the spear of His death on the cross.

But we know that Jesus' new body could do some special things too. Jesus walked into the room where His disciples were hiding with the doors locked, without having to unlock and open the doors. Sometimes Jesus could keep His disciples from recognizing Him in His new body. It seems that Jesus could travel long distances faster in His new body than in His old one. And in His new body, Jesus was able to rise up into the clouds on the Mount of Olives and go back to His Father in heaven.

When the Bible talks about our new bodies—the bodies we will get on the special day that's coming—it talks about seeds and plants and gardens. It says that your old body is like a seed. When you put a seed into the ground, it cracks open and the covering falls off. From way inside, a sprout starts, putting roots down into the soil and putting green leaves up into the air. The sprout isn't anything like the seed: An apple seed is dark brown, small, and oval; an apple sprout has a thick white root that goes down and a thin green shoot that goes up. The white root and greet shoot don't look anything at all like the little brown apple seed. But apple seeds always grow apple trees, not pears or peaches or oranges.

Another picture that the Bible uses to talk about old bodies and new bodies is houses. Being without a body is like being without a house; getting a new body for our spirit, or soul, is like getting a big, beautiful new house with shiny windows, fresh paint, beautiful carpets and drapes and furniture in place of a broken-down, rickety old house with broken windows, dirty walls, no carpets, torn drapes, and worn-out furniture.

Whatever they are going to be like, the pictures the Bible gives us of our new bodies are exciting. What God has planned for us is special and wonderful. It will be like Christmas and birthday and Easter all rolled into one!

God has promised that when He changes our bodies and gives us new ones, He will also change the whole world. Then there will be no dying. There will be no reason to cry. There will be no sadness or grief.

In our world, the way it is now, there is death. Death is an ending. It brings sadness and tears. It separates us from people we love and want to be with. But death is not "The End." Jesus has promised us new bodies, new heavens, a new earth, and a chance to be with Him and with the ones we love. We can believe His promise, because He died for us and rose again.

WHAT IS A FUNERAL?

HAVE YOU EVER been to a funeral? What do you think a funeral is? What happens at a funeral?

When someone dies, that is the end of something. That person will not be part of our lives anymore, or call us on the telephone, or come to visit us. After this, we will have to learn to live without the person who has died.

A funeral after a death is like a period at the end of a sentence. It makes us stop and notice that we have come to the end of something. Many times the funeral is the last chance we have to see the body of the person who died. It is also a time for the friends and relatives of the dead person to get together and remember him. We may talk about the things we remember about our dead friend. We may also talk a little about how things will be different now that our friend is dead.

How does a funeral happen?

When someone dies, the family has to decide what to do with the body. The body can be buried in the ground in a cemetery.

Funerals can be held in a church, at a funeral home, or even in the home of the person who has died. The funeral is planned by the family with the help of the priest or pastor and a person called a funeral director. (A funeral director has other names, too, like mortician or undertaker.)

Usually the body is taken to the funeral home, where it is prepared for being buried. The body is washed and dressed in the clothes it will be buried in. The hair is combed. Sometimes make-up is put on the body, since a dead body doesn't have the normal color a living person has. In preparing a body for a funeral, the funeral director and his helpers use special chemicals to kill germs and keep the body from smelling bad before it is buried.

While the body is being made ready for the funeral, the family will have many things to do too. They must choose a casket—that is, the box the body will be buried in. (It is also called a coffin.) The family may want to choose the clothes in which the body will be buried. They may want to choose special songs, Bible verses, and poems to be read during the funeral service. They may want to ask the pastor or priest to tell special things about the person who died. They also decide where they will have the funeral service—at the funeral home, in the church, or in their own home. They may also choose special flowers for the funeral.

The funeral service usually takes place two or three days after a person dies. Before the funeral itself, there is often a time called a visitation. This is a time when friends of the person who died, his neighbors, and the people he worked with can visit at the funeral home (or sometimes in the church). They come to see the body and to show that they cared about the person who died. At the visitation there is a time for remembering the one who died, talking about the way he lived, and sharing stories about him. A visitation can be a happy-sad time; even though people are sad the person died, they may remember funny stories about him or special and kind things the person did. Although there is sadness because of the death, there can be a happy part, too, in being glad that we had a chance to know this person.

Many people send flowers to the funeral, and these flowers will be around the casket at the visitation and during the funeral services. If there aren't any flowers, it doesn't mean that no one cared about the person who died, though. Sometimes the family will ask people not to send flowers, but instead to give money to the church, the cancer society, the heart association, or some other special organization in memory of the one who died.

Usually the casket is open at the visitation so that the people who come can see the body. This gives the friends of the person who died a chance to realize that the person is really dead and a chance to say "good-by" to him.

Some caskets open up all the way, and you can see the whole body. Many caskets open up only halfway, and all you can see is the head, arms, and chest, down to the waist. The rest of the body is in the casket, but it's covered up.

During the visitation—and later, during the funeral—people may act in many different ways. Some people will be quiet and sad. Some will cry. Other people will talk together and may act as if nothing has happened. Some people will even laugh and joke. This is normal, because people feel their grief in different ways and have different ways of showing their feelings.

The funeral service happens after the visitation. There are many different kinds of funeral services. Some churches have a special funeral service in their prayer book, and this will be used if the family belongs to one of these churches. Other funeral services are very different from a church service.

Most funerals have music. The music might be chosen by the family, and it may be songs that were favorites of the person who died. There are usually prayers and Bible verses. The pastor or priest will pray for the family and friends of the person who died. He will read Bible verses about dying and about heaven. He will usually talk about the person who died, remind us of the kind of person he was, and say how much he will be missed.

After the funeral service there is the burial. At many older churches, the burial ground, or cemetery, is on the church property. Today, however, the cemetery is usually farther away. The casket will be placed in a special car, called a hearse. Then the family and friends will get into their cars and follow the hearse in a funeral procession to the cemetery. Not everyone who attends a funeral service goes to the cemetery; some people go back home or go back to work.

A cemetery is a special place for burying. At the cemetery there will be a grave, which is a big hole in the ground. In the grave, under the ground, is a vault, a special case for the casket.

Usually there is a place beside the open grave with chairs. The casket is placed here before it is put into the ground. The people who go to the cemetery get together for a short service. This graveside service is like the funeral service, only much shorter.

This is usually the end of the funeral. In most places today, the casket is not put into the ground until everyone has left. Later in the day, a special machine comes, lowers the casket into the ground, and closes the vault. Then the grave is filled with dirt again. The funeral flowers may be put on top of the grave. Later on, a marker is put on the grave, with the person's name, the date he was born, the date he died, and maybe a special saying. We usually call this marker a tombstone.

Sometimes the body is not buried in the ground. Cemeteries also have special buildings for caskets. The casket is put into a space in the wall, if the family has chosen to have the person buried in this special building, called a mausoleum.

At times there is a memorial service instead of a funeral service. This happens if the body of the person who dies can't be buried. Sometimes, when people die in an accident or in a war or far away from home, the body can't be buried at home. There may also be a memorial service in the city the person lived in if his body is going to be buried in a different city—for example, the city in which he was born and grew up. Except for the burial, memorial services are very much like funeral services.

When the funeral is over, that is the end. Now it is time to start a new way of living, to learn to live without the person who died. After the ending, there is a new beginning. After we stop, we are ready to make a new start.

QUESTIONS

1. If you have ever been to a funeral, what do you remember about it?

2. Have you ever been to a cemetery? a mausoleum? Are these "scary" places? Why or why not?

SUGGESTIONS FOR PARENTS

If your church has a prescribed funeral service in the prayer book, you might want to go over this with your children, reviewing the parts of the service and the purpose and emphasis of each one.

If your children have shown special interest in this chapter, this might be a good time to arrange a visit to a funeral home, to attend a visitation, or to attend a funeral. You might want to include a trip to a cemetery. Be prepared to discuss how the services you visited are like those described here, and how they are different.

If it seems appropriate for your situation, you should be willing to talk about cremation with your children, especially since cremation is coming into wider use in some places and among some church groups. You may explain that, instead of being buried in a casket, for some people a special process is used that reduces the dead body to ashes. For a person who has been cremated, the funeral service is very much the same as for others, except that an urn—a special jar—with the ashes in it will be at the front of the church in place of the casket. After the funeral service, the urn with the ashes may be buried in the cemetery, or it may be put into a mausoleum. Flowers and a marker may be put over the place where the ashes are buried, just as they are over a grave.

HOW DO YOU FEEL
WHEN SOMEONE YOU
LOVE DIES?

HAVE YOU EVER lost a favorite doll or stuffed animal? Have you ever been sick and had to miss a parade? Has your favorite Christmas present ever broken, maybe even the day after Christmas? Has your mom or dad said you couldn't go to a roller skating party or spend the night at a friend's house? Has your best friend moved or changed schools, so that you don't see each other anymore?

If any of these things has happened to you, how did you feel? You might have felt sad, angry, bored, or some mixture of those feelings. Whenever we lose something that we like, or are disappointed by not getting to do something we wanted to do, we feel "grief." "Grief" is a word used for the sadness and other feelings that come when we lose something or someone that we care about. Grief comes in many sizes—big, little, and in-between. When a double-dip Jamoca almond fudge ice cream cone topples onto the dirty sidewalk, we may feel a "little" grief; when we get a B– on our report card when we wanted an A, we may feel a "little" grief; when a favorite dress or pair of pants wears out or gets too small, and mother says we can't wear it anymore, we may feel grief.

There are many different ways of losing someone we love. Sometimes our best friend decides to be best friends with someone else. Sometimes our favorite teacher gets married and stops teaching school. Sometimes our grandma and grandpa move to another city or a different state, and we don't see them as often. Sometimes our parents get divorced, and mom or dad moves away. Sometimes someone we love dies.

When we lose someone we love, no matter how, we feel grief. Part of grief is sadness. It may be a crying kind of sadness, and we may cry and cry; it might be a kind of sadness that leaves an empty, hurting place inside of us, and we don't cry.

Grief can be more than just sadness, though, especially if it's a "big" grief. It can be an empty feeling, as if the world has turned gray, the way it does when clouds come up and block out the sun at noon. Nothing seems fun anymore, nothing seems worth bothering about, and we might feel tired and bored.

Sometimes grief feels a lot like being very, very tired. It might feel like a lot of work to get up in the morning; getting dressed might be a big job. It might feel easier just to lie in bed. Sometimes grief can make it feel hard to walk or move, and we don't feel like doing anything or going anywhere.

Sometimes grief feels like being afraid. We aren't really afraid or we don't know what we're afraid of, but it feels the same. Our stomachs might get all tied up in knots, and our hearts might be pounding hard; we may find that we are breathing fast and hard, and our mouths and throats are dry.

Feeling angry can be a part of grief too. We may get angry with ourselves and feel as if it's our fault that we lost something we cared about. We might get angry with other people—our mother and dad, our brothers and sisters, the doctors and nurses, or even God.

Grief can make us feel sick to our stomachs. We may not feel like eating; when we try to eat, we might find that there's a big lump in the throat, and we can't swallow. If the grief feels like an emptiness inside, we might find ourselves eating a lot, as if we were trying to fill up the empty place with food.

Grief may make it hard to sit still or stay in one place. We may find that we walk around and around. When we start to read a book, watch TV, do homework, or work on a puzzle, we can do it only a few minutes before we have to get up and move around again. Everything we try seems boring, uninteresting, or too much work.

If the person we loved was someone our mom and dad loved too, we might see our mom and dad grieving. This can be frightening and upsetting. It can make us afraid to see mommy or daddy crying or upset. Sometimes we feel that we don't really know this person who is crying, or angry, or scared, yet this person is mom or dad. When we want to go to mom and dad to have them help us with our grief and comfort us, we might be afraid to make them cry or make them angry. This can make us feel scared, confused, and lonely.

Some people act mean when they are grieving. It seems that they are always picking a fight and getting into trouble. If we feel angry, upset, and empty, we might act mean to other people. Suddenly it seems that everyone is yelling at us! If our grief makes it hard to pay attention or hear what other people are telling us, this can end up with our teachers and our parents yelling at us a lot too.

As you can see, there are many different feelings that might be a part of grief. No one has all these feelings all the time; everyone has his own way of feeling grief, and it's different for everyone. It's a good thing that we don't have to put up with all the possible feelings of grief anytime we lose something or someone we love!

Grief isn't with us all the time, either. At first we may feel our grief almost all the time. After a while we start to feel better. We can sit and read a book; we can get excited about a basketball game; we feel like running or jumping or playing with our friends. We laugh and joke and have fun again. Then something happens that reminds us, and the grief feelings come back. For a while it seems as if our grief is a sneaky monster, waiting until we are feeling happy to jump out and make us feel bad again! Then we may cry again or feel angry, bored, or scared.

When our grief feelings come back, we notice after a while that they aren't as bad as they were in the beginning. We find that our grief is "softening." The other feelings don't last long, either. After a while the grief feelings hardly come back at all and don't last when they do.

While we are getting used to living without someone we loved, we may find ourselves going back and forth between "grief" feelings and "normal" feelings, even four or five times in one day. This going back and forth between feeling grief and feeling normal is part of grieving, but it can be very confusing while it's happening. While we are feeling grief, it's hard to believe that we will ever feel all right again; when we are feeling "normal," it's hard to believe that the grief feelings were real.

As time passes, we get used to living without the person we've lost. Our grief feelings don't come and make us feel bad every time we're feeling good; in fact, they don't come back very often at all, and they usually don't last very long. We may find that they come only at night or on special days like Christmas, birthdays, and special family times. This doesn't mean that we have forgotten the person we loved. We will be able to remember them, and there may even be some sadness with the remembering; however, a lot of the memories will be happy or funny—memories that make us smile or laugh instead of cry and hurt. Things that remind us of our friend, our pet, the person we lost will be able to make us feel good, even if there is a bit of sadness with the good feeling.

Everybody is different; everybody grieves differently. In

a family, some people will grieve loudly, while the grief of others will be quiet and almost hidden. Some people will finish their grieving more quickly than others. There is no "right" way to grieve, nor is there any "right" amount of time for grief to last.

QUESTIONS

1. Can you remember the last time you lost something or someone you cared about? How did it happen? How did you feel?

2. Do you think that you have ever felt "grief"? What did your "grief" feel like?

3. What are some ways people act to show that they are feeling grief? What do you think of these ways of showing grief? Are there any that you use? Are there any that you think you shouldn't use?

4. Talk about the difference between feelings and actions. Can you decide how you are going to feel? Why or why not? Can you decide how you are going to act? Why or why not?

5. If your pet dies, do you think that the person in the family who cries the most is the person who loved the pet the most? (Talk about this in the context of the variety of means we have for feeling and expressing grief.)